THINK
FOR
YOURSELF

A Guide to Changing Your World
by a Man Who Changed Ours

Frank M. Berger, MD

ACB Publishing LLC
New York

About the Book

This book begins with a biography of the author, followed by his intentions for the book, an essay on his approach to living, and a group of personal statements. Then it opens into a catalog of "views on many subjects" that completes the book. The catalog includes 60 topics–from "action" to "work"–drawn from the scores of observations and quotations that filled the author's handwritten notebooks. Readers are invited to think for themselves by testing their views on these subjects against those of the author and those he quotes, who often challenge rather than agree with his conclusions.

The notebooks were edited by Leslie Elliott. Thanks to Sheri Gilbert, Carlisle Hacker, Claudia Jeenel, Wendl Kornfeld, Leslie Kriesel, Rodney Life and Margery Stein for their help in the preparation of the book.

ॐ

A limited number of copies were originally issued under the title
A MAN OF UNDERSTANDING

ACB Publishing LLC
Lenox Hill Station, P. O. Box 1738
New York, NY 10021
Library of Congress Control Number: 2016918813
ACB Publishing LLC, New York, NEW YORK
ISBN: 0997041900
ISBN: 9780997041903

This book would not exist without the tireless support of Dr. Berger's widow, Christine. They met in midlife and were together 33 years before he died. Since during much of that time he was working on the notebooks, she determined they should be published, both as a tribute to him and so the insights and wisdom he had gathered could be shared with others.

‏ও

Writing down one's reflections, not by way of "contributing to literature," but for one's own considered guidance in living.

— MARCUS AURELIUS (121-180)

In our infinite ignorance, we are all equal.

— KARL POPPER (1902-1994)

By diligent attention, by reflection, by temperance, by self-mastery, the man of understanding makes for himself an island that no flood can overwhelm.

— BUDDHA (563-483 BCE)

Contents

Frank M. Berger, MD

1913–2008

Frank Milan Berger came to the United States as a young medical researcher in 1947, bringing with him an idea that changed modern medicine. The excerpt below, from Benedict Carey's New York Times *obituary of March 21, 2008, describes the events that brought Dr. Berger to national attention. Dr. Berger's own reminiscences follow.*

Dr. Frank M. Berger [was a researcher in a London laboratory] ... when he noticed that a chemical agent he was working with had a calming effect on laboratory animals. ... He described this "tranquilizing" action in a now-classic 1946 article in The British Journal of Pharmacology.

He was intrigued, he said later, by the way anxiety seemed to come and go in people without apparent reason: "These people are not insane; they simply are overexcitable and irritable, and create crisis situations over things that are unimportant. What is the physiological basis of this overexcitability?" The answer to that question spawned a billion-dollar industry and transformed the general public's perception of prescription drugs.

After moving to an American firm in New Jersey, Dr. Berger and a chemist, Bernard Ludwig, synthesized a related tranquilizing compound, called meprobamate, and in May 1955 introduced the drug under the trade name Miltown, after a hamlet near their lab.

Sales exploded. Within months, the drug had become the best-selling drug ever marketed in the United States, and pharmacies could not keep it on their shelves. ... Time magazine ran a story about "pills for the mind" ... [and] the comedian Milton Berle started calling himself "Miltown Berle."

... The era of big-time psychopharmacology was under way and similar drugs like Librium would soon capture the public imagination. ... The drug was so successful, and opened up such a wide market, that pharmaceutical companies formed teams of chemists to claim a slice of the pie ... [and] have been competing to create the next blockbuster ever since.*

ॐ

Dr. Berger's recollections have been edited from interviews with Leo E. Hollister in 1995 and Thomas A. Ban in 1999 for the Oral History Archives of the American College of Neuropsychopharmacology in Nashville, Tennessee.

I was born in Pilsen, the famous beer town in what is now the Czech Republic. I went to Czech schools and then to the German University in Prague to study medicine so I could pursue a career in medical research. When I was studying bacteriology there I developed a treatment for cystitis that is still being used. I was about 22 when my findings were published and I had a publication almost every year after that. After graduation I started in research at the Czech equivalent of the NIH.

Then in March 1939, I left Czechoslovakia. My mother was Jewish and people of Jewish origin were no longer welcome. An uncle in America had already sent us the required papers. Hitler came on the 14th, I believe; on the 15th I married my girlfriend and on the 16th got on the train for America with her and my brother. My sister and parents couldn't be persuaded to go. We could take only what bags we could carry and very little money. When we reached the port in Holland we learned the United States had declared all Czech visas invalid and we had only a week before we'd be deported back. We were very fortunate in obtaining entry into England through the generosity of an English Quaker woman I never met. Because of her I'm here today.

It was very difficult in London: I had no money, no friends, no job, and my English was so poor I couldn't get one. To go on public support I would have had to declare myself Jewish, Communist, or Roman Catholic, and I refused to do that. I prided myself on being just a human being and felt I could not adopt a teaching I didn't believe in. I lived on what charities handed out, slept on park benches, and usually ended up at three a.m. on the bricks of a jail floor, which sometimes felt like a gift. But my wife needed shelter and the Jewish Center generously accepted her, though since she wasn't Jewish she was in no danger from Hitler.

So many refugees were flooding into London the government moved us to a camp in southeast England, where I helped the English doctor with refugees' medical needs. Then the Germans began bombing the area and my wife and I were moved to a London suburb, where I did limited medical work at a hospital because refugee physicians were not allowed to work on their own. When that changed in 1941, I took a job in an infectious-disease hospital in Manchester—one of the most interesting periods of my life.

There was a diphtheria epidemic, mostly affecting babies under a year. Finding a vein in such a small child to deliver the antitoxin to save it was very difficult and many, many babies died. The worst part was I had to inform the parents. That was the time I became an agnostic. I felt if the good Lord permits this, a man of character should have nothing to do with that good Lord.

Though I did no research in those years I did learn English, and in 1942 found a job as a bacteriologist in Wakefield, Yorkshire, affiliated with the University of Sheffield. I became interested in penicillin and devised a way to extract it from the liquid it was grown in. I published the method in *Nature*, my first paper in English, in 1944. There was resistance to publishing anything that might help the enemy, but I felt the benefits shouldn't be kept secret. So many lives depended on surviving those infections and there was nothing else to treat them.

British Drug Houses Ltd in London saw the article and hired me to find a non-toxic way to preserve penicillin. One agent we tried was mephenesin, which had a remarkable side effect I'd never seen before. It produced reversible muscle paralysis in lab animals, but they remained fully conscious. Though unable to turn over when put on their backs, their eyes were open, the corneal reflex was present, heartbeat regular and they appeared to follow what was happening around them. After minutes or hours, depending on the dose, there was spontaneous and complete recovery to their state prior to the administration of the drug.

I recognized I had a new non-toxic medication and wanted to do more work on it; then another scientist solved the penicillin problem and our project was stopped. BDH wasn't interested in mephenesin, but I was. I published a paper in the *British Journal of Pharmacology* in 1946, describing it as a muscle relaxant and noting its "tranquilizing" properties, a term I used in the first paragraph.

In 1947 I came to America. At the time one couldn't arrange a job before arriving, but some Americans had read the article and encouraged me. My wife was also very persuasive. Again my uncle sent papers and again, I could take only a small amount of money. Once here, I called the people on my list and within a month was assistant professor of pediatrics at the University of Rochester, where I was able to restart the research.

I'd tried mephenesin on myself and discovered it was safe, and it was also being used in England, but only intravenously, which was impractical. In Rochester I had access to about 200 patients with cerebral palsy, Parkinson's, and other involuntary movements and I tried it on them with fair results. I published the work in the *Journal of the American Medical Association* in 1948, which, to my surprise, was written up in the newspapers. Squibb managed to get the drug approved by the FDA and it became their best-selling drug.

Pharmaceutical firms approached me, but I wanted royalties if I developed a successful drug. Only Carter Products, of Carter's Little Liver

Pills, which had a small subsidiary called Wallace Laboratories in New Jersey, was willing. In 1949 I became their research director.

Their very capable and intelligent chief chemist, Bernard Ludwig, was happy to prepare compounds for me, so we started experimenting. We soon came up with one we called meprobamate. We applied for patents for it and related compounds in 1950. After a year of successful toxicity trials in several species, we began trials with humans through clinicians and psychiatrists in New Jersey and Florida. We had given each compound the name of a nearby town, and "Miltown" was the one we supplied to doctors because it gave the best results.

Carter was reluctant to launch the drug the way I wanted, which even then would cost more than a million dollars, so we made a movie of rhesus monkeys on the drug. They're wild and difficult in the lab but kind and gentle if you meet them in India. The film showed that a monkey on barbiturates was flat out. A monkey on nothing had to be handled with asbestos gloves. And a monkey after meprobamate became friendly and nice, so you could take off the gloves and shake hands. I showed it at a professional meeting in San Francisco in 1955, and people from Wyeth said that when our tests were complete they wanted to license it from us. So I arranged that with Carter at the same time I was getting it through the FDA, which approved it in June 1955.

Before we could come up with a different name, one of the clinical investigators published his findings using the name "Miltown." Wyeth called their brand Equanil and sold twice what we did because doctors liked their name better. Even so, Wallace's annual sales, $80,000 when I arrived, were about $100,000,000 in 1956. Carter Products became Carter-Wallace, was listed on the stock exchange, and I became its president.

Nevertheless, over the years I had big problems with my royalties and spent a good part of time fighting for my rights. The fellow who developed Benadryl antihistamine as a graduate student had become one of the richest men around. But I had signed a document when I was new in America that I did not understand. And once you sign something it is very difficult to modify it. So that is how I failed to become the richest man in America. Since I failed to become the richest, I tried to become the happiest.

Near the end of the '60s, Carter-Wallace installed a new management team and I became head of research only. I worked on a number of new compounds, some of which were developed and introduced to the market, but it wasn't the same. In 1973 I resigned. One of the products in the works was eventually brought out, but in the end they shut down their pharmaceutical operation.

I was 59 when I left and technically I retired but did not start playing golf. I became a consultant to many firms in Europe and this country and participated in developing various immunological products. I was also visiting professor and lecturer at the University of Louisville.

At Louisville I had the opportunity to learn some psychiatry and see psychiatric outpatients. I found it most interesting. My feeling was that most people we saw really had no psychiatric disorders. They had problems of living, did not get along with their spouses or with their children, did not get along with their boss, and had not been taught, had not been educated, had not been prepared, to handle all the crises of life. So they got stressed, broke down, and had to see a doctor, and the doctor did not know what to do. So he put one of the psychiatric names on them. And I don't know what should be done about it.

We need some new breakthroughs in treatment. Research with neurotransmitters is very important, but we're reaching the point where we know as much about them as we need to. We need to explore more intensively the biology of consciousness, learn more about the biology of falling asleep, not just what brain waves show, but also its chemistry. We need a new approach. The discoveries of the 1950s have been milked almost to death.

&

Dr. Berger, who read and wrote in four languages, published over 100 scientific papers during his career. At the same time he was reading constantly and widely in fields far beyond his own. After years of jotting down ideas and quotations on scraps of paper, at 75 he began to copy this wisdom into notebooks so others could share it, adding new information on many subjects and critical lessons he had learned during his own "long, happy and successful life." He continued adding more quotes and ideas, opinions and summaries, as sharply alert and interested in everything as ever, until he died in 2008 at 94.

Dr. Berger and his wife had two sons after they moved to the U. S. She died in 1972, and three years later Dr. Berger married Christine Anderson.

FROM THE NOTEBOOKS

Why Write the Book?

What I have learned during my lifetime is much more important than what I have contributed. For years I was getting ready to write a book that would clearly and simply express any wisdom and understanding I had acquired.

Now that I have been around a long time, more than 75 years, and have gradually discovered how to be happy and successful, I would like to put what I have learned down in writing. Most of it is not original, having been taken over intentionally and unintentionally from others. All I can claim for myself is putting my outlook and views into a framework that may be comprehensible and potentially useful to others.

In my immodesty I want to offer a recipe for happiness and success, though I am aware that this is not the best of all possible worlds. I know quite a bit about the evil, pain, and injustice that surround us and are inflicted upon us. I am not sure that all this will be undone in another life, or that there is life after death. The time is here and now.

❧

We need a guide for everyday life, a set of rules to teach us how to help ourselves so that we might attain, within the limits of our talents, potentialities, and dreams, the success and contentment we desire.

When Maimonides wrote his famous *Guide for the Perplexed* 800 years ago, modern science had not yet been born. Since then many things have changed, but we still have not learned to live more satisfying, more interesting, more enjoyable, and happier lives. Because despite all we do know, we still do not fully understand many things that happen when we observe the world around us—the forces responsible for events or our reactions to them.

There are also the unanswered questions about the origin of the universe, whether God exists, the purpose of life, the mystery of death. We may have found that the advice freely dispensed to us by our educators, by the government and churches, or by physicians and scientists does not always bring about the desired results. Or that the teachings and beliefs of parents and loved ones may not have proven true or helpful. Or that our reasoning minds cannot accept many of the precepts we were taught, or were expected to accept, by those in authority. So one goal of this guide is to liberate you from these perplexities by showing it is possible to live a rewarding life without the answers to the eternal questions.

Instead of giving advice, this book tries to help you understand how things are, not how they are supposed to be or how you would like them to be. It does so in the hope that once you understand how things really are and what is making them so, you will be better able to create conditions and circumstances that will be more acceptable to you.

∂

All my life, whenever I read or heard something that appeared important to me, I wrote it down. I wanted to build up a collection of aphorisms that would help me live a long, happy, and successful life—which I have done, in spite of all that was happening. There were also certain words I wanted to be clear about. What do we mean by "the soul"? What is "art" and why are people interested in it? Whenever I came across a statement that helped me understand such concepts, I made another note. Now I want to share these notes with those who care to read them.

∂

None of us stands alone. Every idea, every invention, every piece of art is based on and originates from a previous idea or accomplishment. In a sense, everything has occurred before and nothing is completely new. That is why I cannot take credit for what is said in this book. I have merely re-expressed what I have heard before when I felt that it was true and beautiful.

An Approach to Successful Living

This essay, evidently drafted as an introduction, was found on its own among the notebooks.

A story has gained currency that the late Gertrude Stein was on her deathbed when she was visited by an admirer. Hoping that the dying Ms. Stein would have a philosophical insight at that special moment, the person asked, "What is the answer?"

On the verge of stepping into the eternal unknown, Ms. Stein replied, "What is the question?"

My outlook on life is rather like hers. Circumstances have taken me to many lands, and, after a career at once focused and wide-ranging, I have concluded that the only response to unanswerable questions like the one presented to her is: ask more questions. Ms. Stein had reached a point, as I have, when the sum of many experiences leads to one certainty: the general uncertainty of all things.

This work is an attempt to share some of the things life has taught me. The most important are not concerned with medicine or science, but with an approach to day-to-day living that has helped me deal more successfully with life's most vexing personal problems.

A Lesson from Childhood

I spent my early life in Prague, now in the Czech Republic. The area had been part of the Austro-Hungarian Empire until after World War I, when it collapsed and a new nation, Czechoslovakia, was born.

A childhood memory from that time has followed me all my life. My mother was Czech and Jewish and my father an ethnic German. As a close and happy family, we knew that language, heritage, and religion need not separate people nor make them enemies.

Alas, that seminal lesson had not been learned by everyone. After the war, people of German heritage like my father were seen as the enemy. There were street demonstrations and I saw violence from the windows of our home. The mob seemed to be in the grip of some delusion that people of different heritages could not live together.

The memory of how destructive that kind of false belief in extreme nationalism can be came back to haunt me devastatingly. At 26 I became a refugee from my homeland during the awful days of burgeoning Nazism. I had qualified as a medical doctor in Prague and was doing research at the International Institute of Health there when I suddenly found myself in a country where my degree was not recognized and I did not understand the language. My new life in England required many adjustments and a serious assessment of my situation. There was good reason, one might say, for me to be depressed and downhearted. Somehow I set about doing the best I could in the face of great difficulties.

Tolerating Uncertainty, Appreciating Small Victories

It was during this time that I began to formulate an idea and an attitude that has served me in good stead ever since. The truth about our lives is that many of the most severe difficulties we encounter do not really have completely effective solutions. We don't have the answers but must act as if we did. Not dealing with situations at all simply aggravates problems to the point where no ameliorating measures can be taken. Wallowing in self-pity is a snowball that can become an avalanche. My solution was to be willing to accept the uncertainty of not having the answers and move forward. I found that learning to tolerate uncertainty, and that we cannot predict outcomes, means that, fully aware of all this ignorance, we can still make decisions, take sides, and behave as if we had answers.

A second crucial truth I discovered about the same time: if you want to be happy, learn to be content with small victories in the daily struggle against the negative aspects of your situation rather than dwelling on its problems. In different terms, our experiences are not as important as how we handle them.

Accepting the Realities

Our contemporary culture seems to be devoted almost entirely to the pursuit of the superficial, even the false. There appears to be a prejudice against dealing with the most basic and significant questions that have always preoccupied intelligent people. Instead, there's a preference for discussing things like popular and cultural events, TV programs, mystery novels, and restaurants. These make up one reality, but we are avoiding what you might call the nonreligious spiritual realities.

Yet, undeniably, we have a spiritual nature that wants to know the unknown. It is impossible to be even reasonably content if we ignore this part of ourselves that looks beyond everyday distractions. Sooner or later, every person who wishes to live fully will have to ask themselves about the existence of a higher power, how the universe came into being, if life has a purpose, and the finality of death.

Other questions without clear answers include: What are morals? Are they universal standards every human should adhere to, or try to adhere to, or do they fluctuate according to circumstance? Do we really have free will or are our lives determined by external causes? What about the fickleness of fortune, the injustice of genetic endowment?

We must also find answers to guide us in conduct, such as: What is right? What is wrong? What is a just social order? What are my rights and obligations as a citizen? What should my attitude be toward religion? How should I conduct my sex life in view of my spiritual nature?

Finally, the question of unhappiness. Many have sought a way out of this impasse through what may be one of the naïve faiths of our time— that our distress originated in childhood conflicts and through protracted psychotherapy we can disable it. But we all had troubled childhoods.

This is not to say psychiatry does not have important functions, but the important thing is to face up to contemporary problems rather than investing in hostility towards the circumstances of our early lives. Accepting what is really so means acknowledging all the realities that now touch our lives, which is much more conducive to finding contentment and reaching one's potential.

Letting Go of Unconscious Beliefs

Even as we are seeking answers, what we already believe influences our lives deeply. Our demeanor and the tranquility of our minds depend on, and are the result of, our beliefs and feelings. We are hardly aware of these beliefs and rarely try to formulate or understand them. Many are based on widespread but utterly false notions—classic fallacies that can be hard to dislodge. Every person who wants to know themselves will also have to deal with these. Some examples you may recognize:

Strength in Numbers A frequent assumption is that if many people believe something, it must be true. In reality, ideas are great or insignificant irrespective of the number of people who believe in them. Think of the tulip mania in Holland in the seventeenth century. Educated, well-to-do people sold their homes and possessions to purchase rare tulip bulbs, believing that the more they accumulated, the richer they would be. The mania would have been comic had it not led to disaster for so many.

"Chosen" People Another common notion is that one ethnic group, one nationality, is inherently superior to others. One's ethnicity and nationality are, of course, accidents of birth and bestow no essential merit upon any individual or group. This particular delusion has led to violence, revolutions, and many wars in the history of the human race.

Father Knows Best Some people imbue all kinds of authority figures with omniscience. Family members, the government, the church are deified. This automatically precludes sensible judgments about many things that impact directly upon a person's life. The aim of those in power, be it one's father, the state, or the employer, is not merely to make the subject obey, but also to make him or her want to obey. This happens because people do not examine issues themselves but rely instead on their leaders' "superior" judgment.

All People Are Born Equal They are not, nor are they equally educable, though all individuals must have equal opportunities and be equal under the law. Even twins educated under similar conditions will differ from each other intellectually, emotionally, and behaviorally.

Tying Self-Worth to Performance Whether considering ourselves or others, our idea of self-worth should not be based on how well or poorly anyone is doing in life, on successes or failures. Like self-acceptance, self-worth must be unconditional. One has to accept oneself as one is—everyone has successes and failures. Performance can be evaluated, but these evaluations must not be related to one's value as a person.

The University Degree There is a myth that educated, cultured, and refined people will behave in a civilized and refined way. We must not confuse culture with compassion. Knowledge of "the humanities" does not necessarily have a humanizing influence.

Seen in the News We often see willingness to accept untruths that appear in the media. Bad news sells media of every kind and people frequently believe it. The problem is that a great deal of the bad news is false, but is never corrected later.

To rid ourselves of such misunderstandings, we have to learn the invaluable art of unlearning, and avoid feelings of guilt when we discard these ideas or beliefs and form our own. If we fail to challenge and let go of fallacies—if, as typical, unthinking members of our societies we become their victims—we are actually courting disaster. Day after day, these passively accepted beliefs can cast us into irrational conflict with others. We can become unable to take even simple steps to help ourselves out of these mindsets. The doors are shut against the vital, thoughtful inquiry necessary to free us to create our own opinions.

Thinking for Yourself

The first step in resolving this is to investigate what we already believe in the many areas of our lives. The next step is to identify where these beliefs came from, checking against possible fallacies or otherwise determining if they are really ours. Then we should figure out why we hold these beliefs, especially in the political and religious domains, to clarify our thinking about the big and "unanswerable" issues. We can then, fully aware, consciously decide if we want to keep any of these views or change them.

Thinking for yourself, instead of letting others do it for you, is not easy. It takes courage. But it will build your confidence on a daily basis and create greater trust in your own decision-making ability. Learning to think for yourself also makes you more aware of who you are. Your well-considered opinions will reflect your own mind and not the opinions and beliefs of others.

You can follow Maimonides' lead in this process. Writing to clarify ambiguous religious texts for "perplexed" worshipers, he "transgressed the Law" by exposing it to the light of questioning—but did so to benefit others. You must be equally willing, for your own benefit, to go beyond accepted dogmas and doctrines or other conventional assumptions that might stand in the way of your progress and understanding.

As to the big questions, though the final answers are not yet in, once you define your attitude toward the unknowable it becomes easier to live without them. However, I believe it is essential to examine the questions.

In a larger context, if we think that this is not the best of all possible worlds and more wisdom is both possible and desirable for everyone, we can and must defend a society that will permit us to search freely for answers. The only acceptable limitation or restriction is the golden rule: we must not inflict on others anything we would not tolerate ourselves, and must not knowingly injure anyone else.

Buddha said, "The man of understanding makes for himself an island that no flood can overwhelm." May this book help you see that it is possible to build such an island without leaving the mainland.

A Few Personal Views

These brief statements appeared throughout the notebooks.

Aim in life: to be *l'homme engagé*—a man of and for his time, who is committed to intelligent and deliberate action in the service of a cause larger than himself.

I do not want to be judged by what I have done in the past, or what I was or have been, but by what I am now.

If I believed in the God of the Bible, there would be one prayer that I would address to him daily: O Lord, grant me the power to end the suffering of human beings.

I am more interested in ideas than events, because ideas will make my life more interesting, more rewarding, and more satisfying than preoccupation with passing events.

I value people over abstract ideas, facts over systems, function over form, matter over manner. What is important is people, not national states, politics, or government policies.

The great landmarks of the last 5,000 years are not physical structures but intellectual concepts: evolution, democracy, philosophy, and the existence of the unconscious.

We must search for a language we can all understand.

I want to distinguish what is not known to me from what is not known to anyone.

There is no absolute truth. An empirical statement must be judged not only on the facts on which it is based, but also on the context in which it is made.

Though there are no absolute values, ethics, esthetics, and logic are not possible without norms or standards to judge the quality of human activities in these domains.

I do not believe in collective guilt or collective responsibility.

I do not live to do business but I must do business to live.

I don't try to duplicate enjoyable experiences. Each is unique.

Human beings are educable. They are capable of behaving in a civilized way as individuals and as groups.

Democracy means even people I dislike and despise have human rights.

You do not need religion to have high moral values.

I have only one prejudice: that there be nothing beyond the inquiry of science. The notion that there is any truth we are not allowed to know is abhorrent to me.

We must have free and open debate on every issue and try to find out how things really are, not how they are supposed to be, believed to be, or revealed to be.

Science and religion, art and technology, reason and intuition, personal and collective, masculine and feminine are not opposites, they are complementary.

I know of no evidence that supports a belief in life after death. When we die our soul or spirit dies with us. There is no rebirth, no rising from the dead, no heaven, no hell, no reincarnation.

The basic attitude:

- This is not a rational world, nor the best of all possible worlds. It should be part of our responsibility to make it more so. Karl Marx said, "philosophers have tried to understand it; the point, however, is to change it."

- Good is good enough. Do not get distracted by seeking perfection, which is unattainable.

- Many of the real problems in our lives cannot be solved, but nothing is to be gained from blaming circumstances or individuals. All that can be done is to learn how to avoid crises and how to handle them if they do occur.

- One day we will be able to understand what is going on in this world. But that day is not near. It took millions of years to reach our present state of development and it may take millions more for us to reach ultimate understanding. Let us be happy while alive on this earth. We cannot be sure of any other existence.

Test Your Views on Many Subjects

I always differed from other people in wanting to have a clearly defined stand on everything, but felt I never knew what I really believed about a problem until I had formulated my thoughts in writing. If I could express it, I would understand it. So now is the time for me to clarify my views on many subjects, in the hope that it might help you clarify your own thinking about them. I will try to select in various disciplines the ideas and points of view that are of general interest, and discuss them in clear, non-technical terms. I will also try to state in clear language what I think, feel, or believe about the problems of the day, about the universe, and about all the unanswered questions.

Notes and Key to Periodical Sources

We endeavored to provide dates of authors and sources of publication for quoted materials but were unable to locate all of them.

(FB) indicates a comment by Dr. Berger related to a quotation.

As he quoted frequently from the following sources, we have abbreviated them in the text as:

JAMA   Journal of the American Medical Association, Chicago, IL
NEJM   New England Journal of Medicine, Boston, MA
NYR   The New York Review of Books, New York, NY
NYT   The New York Times, New York, NY
PBM   Perspectives in Biology and Medicine, Baltimore, MD
TNR   The New Republic, New York, NY

A

ACTION, TAKING RISKS

We must not just react to events, we must shape them.

When we know all the facts, it is often too late to act.

A goal is not a goal unless you put a time limit on it.

Some external force will not solve our problems.

You cannot expect help from anyone, unless you are prepared, first and foremost, to help yourself.

❧

"The great end of life is not knowledge but action."
—THOMAS HUXLEY (1825–1895)

"Don't wander down the path that happens to be there. Go and find the right path."
—FRANK SHANN, MD, *The Lancet*, December 12, 1998

"Nothing will ever be attempted if all possible objections must first be overcome."
—SAMUEL JOHNSON (1709–1784)

"There is no security on this earth; there is only opportunity."
—GENERAL DOUGLAS MACARTHUR (1880–1964)

"Life is a daring adventure, or nothing."

—HELEN KELLER (1880–1968)

"Man cannot discover new oceans unless he has the courage to lose sight of the shore."

—ANDRÉ GIDE (1869–1951)

"It is common sense to take a method and try it. If it fails, admit it frankly and try another. But above all, try something."

—FRANKLIN DELANO ROOSEVELT (1882–1945)

"[T]he Noah rule: Predicting rain does not count. Building arks does."

—WARREN BUFFETT (1930–), Berkshire Hathaway
Chairman's Letter, 2001

"Try not to waste all [your] time on trivia. The hard job is keeping your eye on the big mission and remembering that only you can determine what that mission is."

—DERRICK SILOVE, *The Lancet*, July 22, 2000

"If you are not for yourself, who will be? And if you are only for yourself, what are you? And if not now, when? (FB: Or: If I don't do it, who will do it? If I don't do it now, when will I do it?")

—HILLEL (70 BCE–10 CE)

ADDICTION

People use drugs to induce altered states of consciousness. It is possible that a desire for altered states of consciousness is innate, perhaps even necessary.

Drug abuse should be considered a disease, not a crime. Is punishment an effective deterrent to drug abuse?

Drug use and abuse are ways of coping with stress. The apple—the forbidden fruit—helps man to cope with life, not to cop out. When better or more effective ways of coping with stress are found, drugs are given up.

Addiction is a habit that enables us to do some things and disables us from doing others. Addiction may be good or bad depending on what it enables us to do or disables us from doing, and this may be factual or a matter of expectation.

Addiction is a self-sustaining reaction that spreads as the addictive drug becomes more easily available.

Drug addicts care more for personally oriented values than for socially oriented values. Their drug abuse is an expression of a pattern of compliance and defiance of rules—compliance with rules rejected by the accredited authorities and defiance of rules of established authorities. The only way out is to establish the facts and to understand the cause.

There are those who believe that every social problem must be viewed as an indictment of society and its failure to eliminate the "root causes" of its ills. When it comes to addictive behaviors, we now know why some, albeit not all, people become addicted. We do not know why some people will try a drug and then drop it and others do not try it at all.

Addicts will not get better until they first confront the fact that they are addicts. The families of addicts did not cause and can neither control nor cure the addictive behavior—the disease—of the alcoholic or addict. Alcoholics need some measure of coercion. AA supplies it, through the peer pressure generated at regular meetings with other alcoholics. What helps alcoholics and drug abusers is not so much the 12 Steps (which in essence make the participants confess to their failings and helplessness and invoke the help of a higher power) but the support and the distraction provided by group activities. Self-interest, not self-esteem, induces motivation.

Treatment of chemical dependence can be viewed in two ways: medical and psychiatric. The medical model treats chemical dependence as a primary medical illness characterized by the presence of many psychiatric symptoms that disappear after treatment of the chemical dependence. In the psychiatric model, substance abuse and dependence are treated as secondary symptoms to an underlying psychiatric illness. Alcoholism, drug abuse, and other addictions are seen as signs of mental disturbances. They can be ameliorated or eliminated by social interventions such as group therapy or AA, but these measures do not cure or eliminate the underlying mental disturbance.

Pleasure-inducing substances such as opium or cannabis do so only after they attach themselves to a specific receptor in the brain. A substance has now been isolated from the brain that binds to the cannabinoid and opioid receptors. Two endogenous cannabinoid ligands for the cannabinoid receptor have been identified, but addicts are not satisfied with this. Waiting for a better or best solution, they let the best be the enemy of the good.

Many adolescents do not have a reason not to use drugs. We need to provide that reason.

☙

"If one oversteps the bounds of moderation, the greatest pleasures cease to please."

—EPICTETUS (55–135)

AGING

Aging is passive: what causes aging is being alive.

We tend to measure life in terms of dimension—length—when really life might be much better measured in depth.

There is really no difference between successful living and successful aging. We start aging at birth and our reserves diminish as we get older. At 20 years they may be 15, at 80 years they are 0. The USA is 36th in longevity. The countries with the oldest populations are Japan, Hong Kong, China, and Switzerland.

The human brain does not deteriorate across the board. The neurons do not die in old age, they merely shrink. The process is similar to the decline in muscle mass as we age. T-cell activity diminishes, cancer defense decreases. B12 levels in old age are important.

How you use your mind makes a significant difference: brain cells and other functional cells increase in dimension and activity when they are stimulated.

Resilience, i.e., the capacity of an individual to respond successfully to stress, whether physical (hip fracture) or psycho-social (change of residence, loss of spouse), appears to be an even more important factor than vitality in successful aging. So what we believe and what we think have both positive and negative effects on our physical health.

The problem with aging is being unable to fulfill one's essential needs. The two most important are the need to love and be loved, and to feel that we are worthwhile to ourselves and others. Much of what we call senility is nothing more than the reaction of aged people to isolation.

It is not enough to be near people; it is necessary to be involved with them. Many mental and attitudinal changes seen in old people are not biological effects but the result of slipping into "old people" role playing.

We must not be reduced to our age or to our diseases.

For some, the greatest consolation of old age is the belief that future generations will in some way carry on one's life's work.

ॐ

"Age by itself does not bring wisdom, nor does youth automatically bring a fresh viewpoint: some individuals are born doctrinaire, and others embrace new ideas until the day they die."
—DANIEL E. KOSHLAND, JR. (1920–1987), *Science*, February 19, 1988

"In *Love in the Time of Cholera* (Knopf, 1988), Gabriel Garcia Marquez (1927–2014) says, 'Human beings are not born once and for all ... life obliges them over and over to give birth to themselves.' Marquez shows us ... that aging is simply a process of continuing revelation and discovery, the ability to start again from a fresh perspective."
—J. R. SKELTON and J. A. A. THOMAS, CP, *The Lancet*,
December 9, 2000

"Each individual has a longevity potential, and the purpose of living healthful lives and taking medicines is to try to achieve that potential. However, the prospects for further increasing life expectancy beyond one's inherent longevity potential are slim. ... Therefore the focus of gerontology should be solely on quality of life because [as Lucretius said] '… no matter how long you live, the … time you spend alive is insignificant compared with the infinite time you spend dead.'"

—HOWARD FILLIT, MD, review of *The Quest for Immortality* by S. J. Olshansky and B. A. Carnes, *JAMA*, July 25, 2001

"The ability to adapt quickly to a changing environment, to learn, seems to decline in old age. By contrast … the abilities and knowledge accumulated from experiences seem to be unimpaired and indeed, according to some … improve with age."

—SUSAN GREENFIELD, PHD (1950–), *The Lancet*, October 27, 2001

"An inordinate passion for pleasure is the secret of remaining young."

—OSCAR WILDE (1854–1900)

"The man who works and is never bored is never old."

—PABLO CASALS at 95 (1876–1973)

"The real evil [of old age] is not the decline of the body but the indifference of the soul."

—ANDRÉ MAUROIS (1885–1967)

"What is the joy of getting old if we are compelled to act young?"

—C. E. OGBURN

"At any age, our inner life is what we make it."

—JULIA BESS FRANK, MD, *JAMA*, July 10, 1987

"[Of himself] He is the sort of man who, in his enthusiasm for learning forgets to eat, in his joy forgets to worry, and who ignores the approach of old age."

—CONFUCIUS (551–479 BCE), *Analects*, tr. Simon Leys (Norton, 1997)

AMERICA

The great feature of the American system of government is the separation of church and state.

What I don't like about America (although all generalizations are bound to be wrong):

- Americans prefer form over content. In movies or plays the name and notoriety of the actor is all-important, while the plot matters little. They go to a show to enjoy the acting, not to be entertained or inspired by the ideas of the playwright.

- Popular American culture is built on the principles of intimidation and competition.

- We attempt to find answers to contemporary dilemmas by interpreting the 200-year-old Constitution.

- The United States at present is run on the belief that religious affiliation makes for good ethical and moral behavior. That obviously is not so.

- Society is governed by opinion, not by force; by persuasion— which is different from force; by the gradual increase in the influence of manners rather than the enforcement of morals.

- Humanity by and large appears to be in a state of intellectual collapse. Survival and addiction appear to be the great themes. Sports are a substitute for intellectual activity.

- Things are done because they are healthy, accepted, appropriate, instead of being an end in themselves. We do things like eating and having sex to satisfy the urge instead of for the fun of it.

- Individual lives succeed or fail depending, in unquantifiable measure, on talent and environment.

- Most people today have so few inner resources that they have to look to others to validate their sense of self. They need to be admired for their beauty, charm, celebrity, or power—attributes that will fade with time.

- The American definition of old age: you are old when you have outlived your success.

Victorians believed in work as a way of redemption. Americans favor results.

An increase in antipathy toward the poor, and toward every effort of social amelioration, was characteristic of American life in the 1990s. Aspects of religion in American society: science and dogma cannot coexist; separation of church and state; use of religion to suspend judgment and good sense and to promote anti-intellectualism; pressure to get welfare out of the system and get religion in.

Why are Americans so prosperous? There is no place to sit down. I had never known, until I came to America, that humans as well as horses can eat standing up.

ॐ

"Ideologues believe what is right, works; Americans believe what works is right."

—Mark Shields (1937–)

"After all, the chief business of the American people is business. ... We make no concealment of the fact that we want wealth, but there are many other things that we want very much more. We want peace and honor, and that charity which is so strong an element of all civilization. The chief ideal of the American people is idealism."

—Calvin Coolidge (1872–1933), speech to the American Society of
Newspaper Editors, 1925

"We praise men now, not for the rightness of their cause, but because they care; the primary thing is not truth but concern. This of course puts a premium on fanaticism, not to speak of fakery. ... Many [groups] feel excluded. The premise of these students' concerns is that 'where you come from,' your culture, is more important than where you are going. They are rather like Plato's noble guardian dogs in *The Republic* who love what is familiar, no matter how bad it is, and hate all that is strange or foreign."

—Allan Bloom (1930–1992), *Giants and Dwarfs: Essays 1960–1990*
(Simon & Schuster, 1990)

"Friends and Fellow Citizens: ... Observe good faith and justice toward Nations; cultivate peace and harmony with all. Religion and morality enjoin this conduct; and can it be, that good policy does not equally enjoin it? It will be worthy of a free, enlightened and, at no distant period, a great Nation to give to mankind the magnanimous and too novel example of a people always guided by an exalted justice and benevolence. Who can doubt that, in the course of time and things, the fruits of such a plan would richly repay any temporary advantages, which might be lost by a steady adherence to it? Can it be, that Providence has not connected the permanent felicity of a Nation with its Virtue? The experiment, at least, is recommended by every sentiment which ennobles human nature. Alas! Is it rendered impossible by its vices?"

—George Washington (1732–1799), from his *Farewell Address*, 1796

ANGER AND ENVY

Anger is an important inner signal—a message that you may be hurt, that your need may not be adequately met, that you may not be addressing an important issue, or that you are compromising too much of yourself in your relationship with others.

The pain of our anger unseats the integrity of our self.

Venting anger does not solve our problem. Anger is just a signal that a problem exists.

❧

"Envy, that pain of the soul, as Plato calls it, should never for a moment afflict a man of generous instincts who has a sane outlook in life."

—Sir William Osler, MD (1840–1919)

ART

Everyone needs a kind of second life, a life where one feels comforted, happy, and isolated from problems of everyday living. Poetry, literature, and art permit us to enter that world.

Our culture glorifies art and despises the ordinary and everyday. The culture of the Far East finds beauty in the slightest gesture, the wrapping of a package, the furnishing of a room. It is easy to prefer a work of art to one's morning toast. It is much more interesting to turn one's morning toast into a work of art.

The artist's chief objective is to increase our capacity for perception. The visible phenomena of the world are only one aspect of reality. The artist reaches deep inside himself in an effort to recover another, lost reality and to make it visible on canvas.

One function of art is to arouse people's interest in themselves. It can be a healing force. It can truly revolutionize the way we think, even revolutionize our lives by showing us who we really are—not just animals, and yet the same as animals. Another function is to transmit the preciousness of art.

Art is communication, a way of expressing and communicating perceptions, feelings, or attitudes that cannot be communicated in any other way.

Paintings do not always need a subject to be intelligible or to be a recognizable image of something, such as a person, a place, or an object. They can be a pure distillation of form and color. Like music, they can communicate directly with the emotions without the need for the intermediary of an object. The painting itself is the "thing," not the image of the thing.

Art and science:

- In the analysis of human psychology, art is capable of contributing more than science.
- A work of art can never be surpassed. It is perfect and complete as it is and it does not age. Not so with science: every scientific achievement is only partial and asks to be surpassed and outdated.

The common purpose of the great modern artists has been to explore the boundaries of what is known—which is to say, to experiment with new forms in the hope of extending human consciousness. Anything new is disturbing to the nervous system, but in such cases the shock is a result, not an intention. Critics represent the taste of the audience while the artist follows the imperatives of his vision.

Art is separate from religion. In the past it was used mainly to glorify God. Now it brings fame and glory to man.

The quality of the highest art is such that you are bewitched before you understand the process.

Art is an outlet for suppressed emotions. All art is ultimately about the human condition—about fear, terror, isolation, loneliness, difficulties in communication, powerlessness.

The pleasures and consolations of art—why do we turn to it, or why don't we?

ॐ

"We look at things instead of really seeing them."
—FREDERICK FRANCK (1909–2006)

"The most profitable arts, I say, are those that have most to do with folly, least to do with learning; in other words, those that suit man's natural bent."

—DESIDERIUS ERASMUS (1466–1536)

"Education in the arts, broadly defined, provides an indispensable means of helping us to develop our capacity to see the world and all its objects as crucibles of unexplored meaning. The choice is never between instruct or delight. The arts must always do both. ... Attentiveness and interpretive struggle teaches us one great, overarching lesson: that there is more to most of what we see than meets the eye ... that we often can greatly enrich our lives and the lives of others as well by trying to find out what that 'more' contains."

—PHILIP W. JACKSON (1928–), *PBM*, Autumn 1992

"If art can't be cleanly distinguished from obscenity, as more than 30 years of failed Supreme Court tests make clear, then private consumption of obscenity must be endured so that art can be protected."

—JEFFREY ROSEN (1964–), *TNR*, October 1, 1990

"The purpose of art is not to give pleasure and teach morality but to enrich the human condition."

—GIOVANNI BATTISTA VICO (1668–1744)

"Art does not reproduce the visible; it makes things visible."

—PAUL KLEE (1879–1940)

"I paint things as I think of them, not as I see them."

—PABLO PICASSO (1881–1973)

"Art has to be made up and is, after all, an invention."
—Francisco de Goya (1746–1828)

"Art is something that tells you something that you did not know you needed to know."
—Jerry Saltz (1951–), The New School, New York, April 17, 1995

"To understand a painting one must live with it. The speed of today leaves very few time to really live with anything, even ourselves."
—Arthur Garfield Dove (1880–1946), 1920

The following are by M. Therese Southgate, MD (1928–2013), from her essays in *JAMA* on each issue's cover art:

March 10, 1993: "In its broadest sense, anything is art if the maker (or finder) declares it to be so. ... Fortunately, one need not know how to define its terms before one can experience a work of art."

September 1, 1993: "Because René Magritte's (1898–1967) paintings describe ideas for which words do not exist, it is fatuous ... to attempt to verbalize a meaning. [He wrote,] 'People who look for symbolic meanings fail to grasp the inherent poetry and mystery of the image. ... By asking "what does this mean?" they express a wish that everything be understandable.' One must approach the image [as] a mystery to be looked at, not a problem to be solved."

February 16, 1994: "Kupka was the first purely abstract painter. 'If music is an art of sounds that are not in nature and almost entirely created ... I believe I can produce a fugue in colors as Bach has done in music.' The artist's task is neither to reproduce nor to interpret but to create. What he creates is then not only based on nature but is its own reality. Like music, it is a pure abstraction … enjoyed simply in itself."

March 20, 2002: "There is no single way to look at a work of art: each viewer is, along with the artist, a co-creator of the work. The 'work' of a work of art is to open eyes to possibilities beyond the immediate horizon."

B

BOOKS

I have been fortunate: I have been able to buy all the books I wanted to read.

Most books are not read by those who most need to read them. It is the fate of many good books to be preaching to the converted.

A good and useful book has to not only be a treasure-house of detail but also leave an impression that makes a difference.

∽

"Books are not absolutely dead things, but do contain a potency of life in them to be as active as that soul was whose progeny they are; nay, they do preserve as in a vial the purest efficacy and extraction of that living intellect that bred them."
—JOHN MILTON (1608–1674), *Areopagitica: A Speech For the Liberty of Unlicensed Printing*, 1644

BRAIN, MIND, EMOTIONS, CONSCIOUSNESS

The brain delivered so much more than was ordered in the process of natural selection. It developed an ability and a liking for transcending mundane tasks and went on to conceive and manipulate theoretical and philosophical concepts such as numbers theory and quantum mechanics.

The infant's brain is not a fait accompli. The network of connections from one neuron to another is fine-tuned through use and experience. We are born with faculties which, in biological terms, can be expressed as nerve cells linked in pathways specialized to perform specific functions. Sensory experiences such as sight and smell activate and reinforce specific neuronal pathways.

Our brains construct much of what we take to be objective visual data, that is, much of what we "see" is actually built in the brain. What the eye takes in is matched against records of objects previously seen: the reconstruction is done in a manner consistent with our past experience.

Great thoughts and insights cannot be separated from our feelings. That is where computers differ from brains. Computers store, retrieve, and manipulate information in accordance with the instructions of the programmer. They have no emotions, no judgment, no wisdom, and no insight. Memory chips capture data, not wisdom.

The Mind-Body Problem

Does mind exist as a real entity and can it exert a causal influence over the physical universe? The notion that all matter is merely a manifestation of the mind fails to take into account the mind-body problem. How do brain cells, which are parts of the body, give rise to the experience of seeing and the emotions of love or despair, which occur in the mind? Does consciousness exist outside the realm accessible to the natural sciences? Can neurophysiology provide an adequate account of the nature of consciousness?

In short, how can we both be genetically programmed robotic DNA survival machines and have the extraordinary capacity to transcend these programs? Consistent materialists must argue that wishes, intentions, and so on are as much, or as little, "given" by our genes as any other aspect of our human existence. The interesting thing about humans is, our ability to change what we do is as much part of our biology as how we do what we do.

Proposition to eliminate mind-body duality:
1) Consciousness is caused by processes in the brain.
2) Conscious states are not themselves higher-level features of the brain.
3) Consciousness is something over and above the neurophysiological facts that cause it. It depends on brain processes but cannot be explained by them. There is more to it than neural firing, and it is this more that requires explanation.

An abstract idea has no known physical basis. It may be the product of a highly developed neural network or of something that is not physical and does not require atoms and molecules to fulfill its role. It just needs a biochemical connection to manifest itself.

Anything spiritual must have a material basis. Insight, understanding, and creativity must all have a material basis, but they occur only if the person is in the proper emotional state to assign values to the various facts and observations of entities about which insights are made.

The soul is one of the manifestations of the brain, perhaps the most important, the most human.

It is possible to measure many physiological correlates of emotional responses using methods derived from natural sciences and clinical research. However, it is not possible to evaluate in an objective way—to measure—the feelings, or emotional responses, experienced by the individual.

❧

"The brain remodels itself as it encounters the world. Brain cells devoted to controlling the left arm, for example, will be assigned another function if that arm is amputated. The number of brain cells assigned to controlling the fingers will increase the more one practices piano ... the brain is built by behavior, even as behavior is predisposed by the brain."

—DAVID W. MURRAY, *The Sciences*, July/August 1995

"What we really need to know [to understand consciousness] is 'how a subjective sensation is caused by something objective ... consciousness is not about learning and memory. The building block of consciousness is emotion.'"

—SUSAN GREENFIELD, PhD (1950–), quoted by Jane Bradbury,
The Lancet, December 12, 1998

"The dominant picture of mind since the Renaissance ... is the tabula rasa: the blank ledger upon which the environment leaves its traces as the mind is given whatever structure and content it finally possesses. ... [Then] in the 1960s Noam Chomsky ... argued persuasively that the human faculty of language is innately structured. ...[J]ust as we do not learn to have arms and legs and kidneys, but have these organs as a matter of our innate endowment, so our mind is best understood as an organized collection of innate cognitive faculties or modules, among which language is one. We acquire a language by virtue of the prior

linguistic knowledge coded innately into our brains, not because our brains are empty receptacles equipped merely to retain the traces of the linguistic inputs they have received."
—COLIN MCGINN (1950–), reviewing *How the Mind Works* by Steven Pinker, *TNR*, February 23, 1998

"We should not treat our ignorance of the nature of biology's role in psychological functioning as evidence that biology in fact has no role."
—D. O. HEBB (1904–1985), *Organization of Behavior* (Wiley, 1949)

"There has to be a unifying force at work between form and matter, that is, there has to be an impulse of play, because only the oneness of reality and form, of chance and necessity, of suffering and freedom, does full justice to the concept of man."
—FRIEDRICH VON SCHILLER (1759–1805), "On the Aesthetic Education of Mankind—Letter 15"

"The idea of the brain as a computer remains just a metaphor. It cannot be taken literally. There is no more reason to suppose the brain is a computer than to suppose that the liver or the gut is one. One can model some of the activities of the brain or the liver on a computer just as one can model the weather on a computer; but that does not make us think that the weather is a computer."
—JOHN R. SEARLE (1932–), *The Rediscovery of the Mind* (MIT Press, 1992)

"One thing people don't realize is that the human brain is not a steady-state system. It's cyclic. Sometimes people are depressed and sometimes they are up—and that's more predictable than you would think."
—PAUL MACRAE MONTGOMERY, Interview in *Barron's*, April 8, 1996

BUSINESS, MANAGEMENT

Businesses should be managed so that they benefit the clients and customers whom they serve, not solely to maximize profitability for the owners.

Adam Smith (1723–1790) wrote that when businessmen get together for even the most innocent purpose, their meeting will inevitably turn into a conspiracy against the public. This is regrettable, not only because there is no business like repeat business but also because it leads to antibusiness sentiments and totalitarian forms of government.

Your mission statement must focus on what you want to be and do. Do not be a product of top-down decision making.

People, including professionals, should be judged by their ability, not by their credentials.

In situations where human relations are involved, such as in the family or in business, competition, comparisons, and judgments of persons are not helpful. Instead of competition, there should be collaboration, and instead of comparing individuals and pointing out differences between them, all should be made to feel included in the group and equally valuable. Also, people should be accepted as they are and not be judged. Some people cannot be accepted, and if they cannot change, they have to be released.

Appreciate; don't criticize.

২৩

"One can conquer on horseback but must dismount to rule."
—GENERAL YEH-LU CHUTSAI (1189–1243) to Genghis Khan

"Be decisive, address issues quickly and deal with the world the way it is, not the way you wish it were."
—JOHN T. CHAMBERS (1949–), President and CEO, Cisco Systems

"We must search for consensus, and not confuse consensus with unanimity. Differences will exist, but the critical need is to identify those core principles with which all interests can agree, and upon which action can be taken."
—JON ROUSH, President, The Wilderness Society

"Companies don't die of serious illnesses, they die of indigestion."
—DAVID PACKARD (1912–1996), co-founder of Hewlett-Packard

"The profit motive is not dominated by greed. It is simply the best yardstick for success and for judging managers. Trust your subordinates. If you cannot approve their recommendations without a careful scrutiny of their memos, you are wasting your most valuable asset, your time. Get rid of those you cannot trust."
—JEAN-LOUIS SERVAN-SCHREIBER (1937–) French journalist and politician

"Rule 23: Give everyone credit. We have been told since potty-training that you get the gold star for individual achievement but it is only so far that individual effort can take us. You cannot do it all yourself. You have to have people who will work on your ideas. And they will do it only if they know that they will get credit for what they do."
—DONALD COFFEY, PHD (1932–), Johns Hopkins School of Medicine

"Conflicts of interest can be avoided only if people recognize a common interest other than self-interest."

—GEORGE SOROS (1930–), *TNR*, September 2, 2002

"Entre le potage et le fromage, on fait du courtage." (Between soup and cheese, we trade.)

—FRENCH SAYING

C

CHOICES AND CHANGES (SELF-TRANSFORMATION)

Choices

Life enhancement is our only and constant goal, and the exercise of choice is our only given means to do so.

Your choices define you, not your origins. Your life is your own, nobody else's.

Individual self-realization is more important than inherited tradition.

What we see when we look in a mirror is a synthesis of our identity, our uncertainties, and our desires.

Social scientists focus on the means by which individuals create order for themselves out of a disorderly world. We construct our own reality.

You are as good as the best thing you have ever done, not the last thing you have done.

❧

"Success: A process of becoming who you already are."
—FRANK POTTS (1903–1990)

"If you are able to be yourself, then you have no competition. All you have to do is get closer and closer to that essence."

—Barbara Cook (1927–)

"First one creates an image of a self, and then one spends a lifetime growing into it."

—M. Therese Southgate, MD (1928–2013), *JAMA*,
September 15, 1993

"First is, be yourself. Nobody else can do that. Second is, don't let the fear of making mistakes keep you from finding out what you can accomplish. And third is, keep learning—continue your education—throughout life."

—Ray Fuller (1935–1996)

"I have learned that you can inherit loyalties, indignations, a temperament, the line of your cheekbones, but you cannot inherit yourself. You must make your life with your own hands, here and now, alone or with others. There will be no sign, no deliverance, no imperative in the blood. You cannot inherit any purpose."

—Michael Ignatieff (1947–), *The Russian Album* (Picador, 2001)

"Early experience, social learning, or choice [cannot be] pitted against biology ... the brain is the product of early experiences, social environment, and genetic instruction. So, it manifests the workings of both nurture and nature ... [which] can be enduring and resistant to change ... [but] need not be inexorable. ... Choice may be a forceful biological process in its own right."

—Dr. Thomas A. Schoenfeld, Letter to *Science*, November 1, 1991

"Every man is the son of his own works."

—Miguel de Cervantes (1547–1616), *Don Quixote*, 1605

Changes

To change the course of our lives we do not need new talents, new capabilities, other circumstances and other opportunities. All that is needed to bring about the change is a new and more sensitive appreciation of all the facts already in existence.

There are only three ways in which a situation can be changed or one's world can be changed: 1) by changing the reality of it; 2) by changing the perception of it; or 3) by changing the way of handling it.

The self-help industry: There is a 12-step program ready to rescue you. Most of the recipes of the so-called "human potential movement for personal self-actualization" are prescriptions for personal and spiritual sloth. From cradle to grave life is to be avoided by therapies. It is all organized life avoidance. In his biography of Werner Erhard, founder of est, Bill Bartley (1934–1990) said, "The problem with most awareness movements is that they make statements that do not appear to have meaning, e.g. 'est is a training program in the expansion and transformation of consciousness.'" (*Werner Erhard: The Transformation of a Man, The Founding of Est,* Clarkson Potter, 1978)

☙

"Our chief talent is the power of suiting ourselves to different ways of life. To be tied and bound of necessity to one single way is not to live but to exist."
—Montaigne (1533–1592)

"To change and to change for the better are two different things."
—German proverb

"The greatest discovery of my generation is that human beings can alter their lives by altering their attitudes of mind. As you think, so shall you be." (FB: Most people don't think.)

—WILLIAM JAMES (1842–1910)

"Nothing in progression can rest on its original plan. We may be as well to think of rocking a grown man in the cradle of an infant."

—EDMUND BURKE (1729–1797)

CREATIVITY

One of the basic freedoms should be to have the right to question and test received information.

The freedom and the courage to be alone is the secret of creativity.

❧

"Don't compete. Create. Find out what everyone else is doing and then don't do it."

—JOEL WELDON

"A man who follows another not only finds nothing, he is not even looking."

—SENECA (4 BCE–65 CE)

"The conventional view serves to protect us from the painful job of thinking."

—JOHN KENNETH GALBRAITH (1908–2006)

"The uncreative mind can spot wrong answers but it takes a very creative mind to spot the wrong questions."

—Sir Antony Jay (1930–2016)

"There is a need to protect original thought: originality can easily be dismissed as deviance, particularly when it conflicts with established opinions."

—W. E. Ormerod, *The Lancet*, June 1, 1991

"New ideas cannot be reached by logic alone. … The mind can only see what it is prepared to see. There has to be the ability to create new concepts … to design a new way forward or around. … Release from fear and inhibition will … not significantly alter the preformed pattern of the brain. To be effective, challenges, alternatives, and provocations have to be set up. Lateral thinking: the generation of new ideas and the escape from old ones."

—Edward de Bono (1933–), *Serious Creativity* (HarperBusiness,1993)

CRIME, VIOLENCE, NONVIOLENCE

There are three psychological traits, or dimensions, of personality, which are often assumed to be interrelated. These express themselves by neurotic, psychotic or criminal behavior. Neurotic behavior, or neuroticism, expresses itself by groundless or irrational anxieties and fears and/or by excessive depression or excitement. A psychotic suffers from delusions and hallucinations and has difficulty differentiating between the real and the imagined. The criminal has lost respect for others. He is driven to violence and does not experience guilt feelings after committing irresponsible and violent acts. These three forms of behavior are present in varying degrees in every individual but not everyone is capable of very violent acts, even in the heat of passion, no matter what the provocation.

Is human destructiveness—violent behavior—reactive to abuse and humiliation (in childhood) or is it innate? It is a law of human nature that what enters as experience exits as behavior.

Violence is symptomatic of deeper social ills. Those who commit violent acts have reasons for their actions.

A person who commits a crime under the influence of drugs is responsible for his action. Using drugs does not itself excuse crime. Behavior may one day be traced to chemical reactions in the brain, but our intentions may affect these chemical reactions.

The law insists that behavior be punished only when it is a matter of "choice." The criminal law looks to intent, not motive. The law should ask what happened, not why. Personal and social behavior are the overt manifestations of intent.

Having a mental disease—a psychiatric diagnosis—should not be considered exculpatory. People can be mentally ill but guilty of a crime in the same way as a diabetic or tubercular patient can be guilty of a crime. Mental illnesses do not differ in kind from other illnesses.

Intimidation and threats do not work. All appeals to tradition or authority fail in practice when there is no consensus about what the traditional categories are or should be.

Good education and a good job do not guarantee that an individual will not be a criminal.

The "tough on crime" policy has been an economic and social disaster.

Human rights groups condemn execution of prisoners with mental illnesses. All executions should be stopped. There is no correlation between the death penalty and the incidence of murder.

The only freedom of the condemned is refusal of consent.

❧

"[Capital punishment] is barbaric; it denies the possibility that people can change; and revenge killing can't erase the original harm."
—JACKIE LEACH SCULLY, *The Lancet*, Lifeline, September 21, 2002

"There is no such thing as an acceptable level of violence … domestic violence applies to both women and men, and can take different forms, not only physical but also verbal and emotional abuse, threats, economic abuse, isolation, social control, pornography and rape … the prevalence and acceptance of violence and violent role models in popular entertainment on TV, in cinemas and the internet, erode inhibitions against violence in real life."
—KAREN BIRCHARD, quoting a Joint Document on Domestic Violence issued by two commissions of the Catholic Church in Ireland, *The Lancet*, September 9, 2000

"About the effects of TV violence … aggressive kids are more likely to watch shoot-em-ups. That says nothing about cause and effect … [but] most of the studies on the subject show some correlation between violence on TV and the real thing: those who watch violent shows tend to be more violent. What they question is whether the watching causes the doing."
—*The Economist*, September 13, 1994

"Violent behavior is not innate or biological: rather it is learned. We learn behavior by observing others. Thus television is a powerful teacher of violent and silly behavior."
　　　　—SHERVERT FRAZIER, MD, *Psychotrends* (Simon & Schuster, 1994)

"Violence, once turned to, is as cruel to the user as it is to the one who suffers under it—both, in different ways, are turned to stone."
　　　　　　　　　　　　　　　　　　—SIMONE WEIL (1909–1943)

"The only purpose for which power can rightfully be exercised over any member of a civilized community against his will is to prevent harm to others. His own good, either physical or moral, is not a sufficient warrant."
　　　　　　　　　　—JOHN STUART MILL (1806–1873), *On Liberty*

"Catching, not convicting, criminals is the biggest problem facing British police and prosecutors. Only 12% of recorded crimes ever lead to a court case. Once in court, more than 90% of cases result in conviction."
　　　　　　　　　　　　　　—*The Economist,* January 29, 1994

"Judges and juries, unlike television viewers and victims, must decide guilt on the basis of reason rather than emotion, and punishment on the basis of public values rather than private rage."
　　　　　　　　—JEFFREY ROSEN (1964–), *TNR,* April 17, 1995

"The justice viewpoint focuses on past behavior as a guide to action. The sentence must reflect the crime, not a possible outcome. However, prediction in the individual case is always uncertain. Treatment failed to prevent juvenile delinquency."
　　　　—JOAN MCCORD (1930–2004), *American Psychologist,* March 1978

"A penal system based on reform did not reduce recidivism."
　　　　　—SIR MICHAEL RUTTER, MD (1933–) and HENRY GILLER,
　　　　Juvenile Delinquency: Trends and Perspectives (Penguin, 1983)

"I have no doubt that behind every crime a personal tragedy lies hidden."

—ALICE MILLER (1923–2010), *For Your Own Good*
(Farrar, Straus & Giroux, 1984)

CULTURE

Culture is the sum total of ways of living, and of the perception and meaning of ideas, that are built up by a group of human beings and transmitted from one generation to another.

Without culture, life cannot be enjoyed to the full. Culture is an indispensable element of life, a dimension of our existence, as much a part of man as his hands. It is *not* some sort of ornamental accessory for the life of leisure.

The main function of a university is the teaching and transmission of culture. It should limit the influence of the barbarism of specialization.

Culture in its broadest sense is the sum of various learned traditions.

❧

"Culture [is] the pursuit of our total perfection by means of getting to know, on all the matters which most concern us, the best which has been thought and said in the world and, through this knowledge, turning a stream of fresh and free thought upon our stock notions and habits, which we now follow staunchly but mechanically, vainly imagining that there is a virtue in following them staunchly which makes up for the mischief of following them mechanically."

—Matthew Arnold (1822–1888)

"Was there ever a nation on God's fair earth civilized from the bottom upward? Never; it is, ever was and ever will be from the top downward that culture filters."

—W. E. B. DuBois (1868–1963), 1903

"An age or culture is characterized less by the extent of its knowledge than by the nature of the questions it puts forward."

—François Jacob (1920–2016), *Of Flies, Mice and Men* (Harvard University Press, 1998)

"Wisdom and understanding ... are reached through a higher kind of discipline than that of reading, which is often but a mere passive reception of other men's thoughts ... .The chief object of culture is not to fill the mind with other men's thoughts ... but to enlarge our individual intelligence, and render us more useful and efficient workers in the sphere of life to which we may be called."

—Samuel Smiles (1812–1904)

"What you have as heritage, take now as task; for thus you will make it your own! Vindicate tradition!"

—Goethe (1749–1832)

D

DEATH, IMMORTALITY

Everybody wants to go to heaven but nobody wants to die.

It is not how a man ends up, but how he affected the lives and thoughts of those around him, of his family and friends.

The purpose of facing death is not to die but to live more fully.

Artur Lundkvist suffered a massive heart attack in 1981 when he was 75 years old. He was unconscious for six weeks, recovered completely, and died 10 years later. He recorded the strange and vivid journeys he had taken during his long coma. Lundkvist remained an unrepentant secularist.

&

"A life full of radiant days—do not weep that it has ended but smile that it has been."
—CONFUCIUS (551–479 BCE), *Analects*, tr. Simon Leys (Norton, 1997)

"A free man thinks of nothing less than of death, and his wisdom is a meditation not of death but of life."
—SPINOZA (1632–1677), *Ethics*

"Is there an afterlife? Either there is nothing—what peace! Or something—how exciting! Let's wait and see."
—JAN STJERNSWARD (1936–), *The Lancet*, October 27, 2001

"Non omnis moriar!" (Not all of me shall die!)
—HORACE (65–8 BCE), at the end of his odes,
which he expected, correctly, would survive him

"Some people who were close to dying but returned to life found for several days everything magnificent. When they again became accustomed to living, the sparkle, astonishment and beauty disappeared. If we could only recognize the proximity of death and the precious gift of life, one would live a full life."
—SOGYAL RINPOCHE (1947–), *The Tibetan Book of Living and Dying*
(HarperSanFrancisco, 1992)

"What we can learn from dying people: we can learn about dignity in the face of indignity, about living life while being stalked by death, about fighting battles no one knows how to win."
—PHYLLIS L. SPECHKO, RN, *JAMA*, February 15, 1985

"We can do nothing about dying or living—except to do it well."
—WILLIAM PFAFF (1928–2015), *International Herald Tribune,* June 9, 1994

"Do not worry too much about dying. It is enough to live and love as best you can. ... Accept death as a fair price for life."
—FORREST CHURCH (1948-2009), *Life Lines* (Beacon Press,1997)

"Don't die before you're dead."
—YEVGENY YEVTUSHENKO (1930–2017)

DILEMMAS OF MODERN LIFE

Why are we unhappy? We are led to believe that we live in the best of all possible worlds. How can you improve on perfection? Therefore everything has to continue as it is. And we all both know and do not believe that everything will continue as it is.

Whether you want to understand the workings of the brain, discover a treatment for an incurable disease, or make a fortune on the stock market, you are confronted with the same problem: You have to construct a complete answer on partial information. Since we cannot predict the future, we have to have a philosophy that will stand up under almost any circumstances. We have to start and work with what is, not with what we would like it to be.

According to James Q. Wilson (1931–2012), "the problems of advanced capitalist democratic societies are not economic at all, they are political and cultural." He says problems such as high crime rates, school dropouts, and drug abuse arise from three causes: prosperity, freedom, and democracy. Prosperity, because the high standard of living extends to the criminal as well as the non-criminal. Guns replace knives and drugs become affordable, but what produces the good life for the individual does not produce it for cities. Freedom, because self-expression is valued over self-control. Democracy, because people expect that government should spend more on education, health care, crime control, and environmental protection while at the same time maintaining a balanced budget and lower taxes. This cannot be achieved by the assumed solutions of waste reduction or elimination of fraud and mismanagement. (*Forbes*, September 14, 1992)

French philosopher and writer Georges Bataille (1897–1962) argued that if an organism's *excess energy* (that is, the energy not used simply for maintaining life) isn't completely absorbed in its growth, as it seldom is, this energy "must be spent, willingly or not, gloriously or catastrophically," including on such activities as war. Thus it is not scarcity and necessity that present living matter and humankind with their most basic problems, but rather excess, luxury, and exuberance. Sex, sports, and hobbies are the usual ways for dissipation of excess energy.

This is not the best of all possible worlds:
- Progress is possible only if you question the established order and beliefs, and try to separate fiction from fact.
- Charity will not solve the problem of poverty.
- Religion will not establish morality.
- Arming will not prevent war.
- The courts and prisons will not eliminate crime or make this a just world.
- Abolition of chemical, bacteriological, or nuclear warfare will not bring peace. Attempts to introduce lesser evils to avoid greater ones usually fail.
- The only hope for a better life is education, but education remains effective only if you retain an open mind and proceed honestly and with integrity.

☙

"In the long run, [J. B. S.] Haldane and Einstein said, ethical progress is the only cure for the damage done by scientific progress

…The ethical problems arise from three 'new ages' flooding over human society like tsunamis. First is the Information Age … driven by computers and digital memory. Second is the Biotechnology Age … driven by DNA sequencing and genetic engineering. Third is the Neurotechnology Age … driven by neural sensors and exposing inner workings of human emotions and personality to manipulation … They will tend, as [G. H.] Hardy said eighty years ago, to accentuate the inequalities in the existing distribution of wealth. … The widening gap between technology and human needs can only be filled by ethics."

—Freeman Dyson (1923–), *Imagined Worlds*
(Harvard University Press, 1998)

"Economic and material goods are no compensation for social and moral ills. … [But this violates] the idea of progress that is so much a part of [the American ethos]: that material and moral progress are the necessary by-products of a free society, an expanding economy, a mobile social structure, a diverse and highly accessible system of public education."

—Gertrude Himmelfarb (1922–), *Forbes*, September 14, 1992

"The greatest fear we are facing is the destruction of civil society by the postmodern acceptance of the degraded, banal, and vicious as amazing, normal, or cool."

—Mark P. Haggard, *The Lancet*, November 10, 2001

"We have to abandon the arrogant belief that the world is merely a puzzle to be solved, a machine with instructions for use waiting to be discovered, a body of information to be fed into a computer."

—Vaclav Havel (1936–2011), speech at
World Economic Forum, February 1992

"In Plato's *Gorgias,* Plato and his opponents agree that the mass of citizens are incompetent to make reasonable decisions on justice and public policy. They must be convinced by rational arguments and guided by the authority of experts. But it is not the truth that makes you free. It is your possession of the power to discover the truth. Our dilemma is that we do not know how to provide that power."

—RICHARD LEWONTIN (1929–), review of Carl Sagan's
The Demon-Haunted World, NYR, January 9, 1997

E

EDUCATION

Education's highest aim is freedom to inquire: what you have not taught me, you have taught me how to learn.

Purposes of education:
- To become wise. It is not the accumulation of knowledge and information.
- To present the problems and unanswerable questions we all have to face, and inculcate in those to be educated the attitude, knowledge, and wisdom that will permit them to live satisfying lives.
- To teach children how not to harm themselves or others and how to live happily.
- To make pupils aware that the rich and powerful do not have all the answers. That riches and power do not necessarily lead to personal happiness and contentment.
- To teach people to understand the machines, techniques, and underlying concepts on which they depend.
- Not so much to impart knowledge but to give people the desire to understand and to learn.
- To make people aware that they have in them the potential to adapt to, and deal adequately with, the strains and stresses of living and the unforeseeable catastrophes to which they may be exposed.
- To promote the attitude of the mind that can distinguish between the important and the urgent, and the desirable and

the attainable, and recognize that both can, but need not, be the same.

- To foster creativity and the ability to communicate.

Learning depends to a large extent on the manner in which the material is presented. It has to arouse and sustain interest. Education should be exploration that fosters zest, self-confidence, curiosity, and trust.

Paradoxically, learning is also learning *not* to think about operations that once needed to be thought about, e.g. learning to speak a foreign language or to play tennis. So learning has two phases: 1) acquiring knowledge of subject; 2) learning to use it unconsciously.

To be civilized, truly educated, and cultured does not require knowledge of the classics, of philosophy, music, art, or literature. It does not need religious faith or familiarity with science. It needs a respect and understanding for:
1) the sanctity of life;
2) the dignity of human beings;
3) the fact that helping and serving others has a higher priority than personal gratification.

Do not let your attitude prevent you from learning enough to be informed.

A student and a scholar may have an equal knowledge of their subject. The difference? Scholars make judgments.

Precepts for consideration when educating oneself or children: Distrust pronouncements by those in authority and in power, and at the same time try to get on with them. Those in power may mean well, but their judgment should not be trusted because they may not know or may lack understanding or be prejudiced.

What do you mean when you say he has no talent? Teach him talent.

Humanities are not about what we should do. They are about what people liked to do.

The humanities are not defined by the subjects they cover—philosophy, religion, the fine arts, or foreign languages—but by the approach taken to the subject. Mathematics, physics, and biology belong to the humanities when they are examined philosophically in the manner of a generalist. History, poetry, and philosophy do not belong to the humanities when they are studied in the manner of specialist scholars.

ॐ

"Education is learning to feel pleasure and pain about the right things. A well-educated man is one who can sing and dance well."
—PLATO (427–347 BCE), *The Laws*

"Education is what survives when what has been learned has been forgotten."
—B. F. SKINNER (1904–1990)

"The Government's greatest failure has been the education of our children. We may become the first developed society to produce new generations less knowledgeable than their predecessors. We are producing a generation of undisciplined illiterates which cannot expect to lead the nation or the world. In the past our strength depended at least in some measure upon the weakness of others around the world."
—AMERICAN INSTITUTE FOR ECONOMIC RESEARCH,
Research Report, February 7, 1994

"Hemingway said that to be a great writer a person must have a built-in shock-proof crap detector ... [a] function of the schools in today's world: a continuing struggle against the veneration of 'crap.'"
                    —NEIL POSTMAN (1931–2003) and CHARLES WEINGARTNER,
                              Teaching as a Subversive Activity (Dell, 1971)

"The beginning of education lies in imitation—wherefore pick someone worth imitating."
                              —MARTIN H. FISCHER, MD (1940–)

"That was the real therapy—the struggle to enlarge yourself to take in a mind greater and more powerful than your own. That task is as difficult for white males as for blacks, for men as for women."
        — DAVID DENBY (1943–), quoted by Joyce Carol Oates in her review of
                              his *Great Books, NYT,* September 1, 1996

"Any piece of knowledge I acquire today has a value at this moment exactly proportionate to my skill to deal with it."
                              —MARK VAN DOREN (1874–1972)

"Americans are obsessed with sports and sports came to be intimately connected with our schools. Sports need not be an ennobling experience. Far from building model citizens, competitive team sports tend to foster selfish motives and antisocial behavior."
        —ANDREW MIRACLE and C. ROGER REES, *Lessons of the Locker Room*
                                                      (Prometheus, 1994)

In a letter to *Science* (August 22, 1986), D. F. Magee said that U.S. elementary schools "devote enormous resources to underachievers, all to the good, but virtually ignore the above average (who are also hard to teach if we are to retain their interest in schooling). ... Decline could be stopped if the United States were willing ... to abandon some ingrained dogmas such as that school systems be under locally elected school boards … and that anything other than private initiative and free enterprise produces parasites. … This country shows a special neglect for its gifted children."

"One can't think because one is learning too much."
—J. ROBERT OPPENHEIMER (1904–1967), discussing Princeton's
Institute for Advanced Studies, May 20, 1960

"They know everything. Unfortunately they don't know anything else."
—FRENCH SAYING about graduates of *les grandes écoles*
(France's elite colleges)

"Human history becomes more and more a race between education and catastrophe."
—H. G. WELLS (1866–1946)

"Studies teach not their own use; but there is a wisdom without them, and above them, won by observation."
—FRANCIS BACON (1561–1626)

ETHICS, MORALS, VALUES

Although they have distinct meanings, these words are often used interchangeably. The essential question in all of them is whether a man's ideas should be judged by his actions. The answer is yes— we have to treat ourselves as responsible and blamable for immoral behavior (and to be restrained from repeating it) when we think of ourselves as members of a moral community. However, when we try to figure out how to make ourselves and our children better people, we tend to view our actions as determined by causal forces instead. But our moral accountability cannot be offset by blaming parents, our enemies, society, mental disturbances, or God. The fundamental teaching goes: I am responsible for my actions and I must accept their consequences.

Common sense tells us that there are no transcendental higher powers that care about our fate. It also tells us that the tasks society assigns to us are not necessarily desirable or beneficial to us or others—e.g., army service, extermination or subjugation of whites, blacks, women, or Jews. So our first duty is not to obey orders but to be skeptical about them.

Ethics

Ethics are related to behavior. Governing appropriate conduct in the moral sphere, ethics are based on what an individual or group has judged to be right or wrong. They are expressed in the way issues are approached, choices made, and action taken.

Morals

Morals: life-enhancing, protecting human existence from the dark forces of chaos. Morals relate to the capability of making a distinction between right and wrong in conduct. They are the norms for right behavior and stand above individual preference in the community.

We all need moral guidance, but it should be based on truth and knowledge, not on religious tradition.

In the settling of moral issues in daily life, the relevant qualities and abilities are: 1) treating others as equals (equality); 2) being aware of one's own and other people's feelings (mutual respect); 3) being able to form one's own principles of behavior in the light of the facts (self-regulating morality); 4) being able to translate these principles into action.

Values

Values are individuals' judgments about what is important, what each of us believes is right or good. What we value and what we believe are more powerful forces in determining who we are as persons than our biological makeup. Our values are intrinsic to how we view the world and interact with it. They set the guidelines within which information and actions are meaningful. What is good and what is bad is predicated for each individual on the values he believes in.

Values are very personal and can fluctuate along a continuum according to circumstances, with only the decisions at the extreme ends being easy.

Conscience is just as much an expression of our own values as it is the voice of values of others that we have adopted.

Values are often only partially justifiable on logical grounds because facts cannot logically generate value judgments.

જ્જ

"Things matter to us for the values or emotional commitments they express, not simply for their practical or material usefulness."
—ROBERT NOZICK (1938–2002)

Ethical Principles

There are three general categories—religious (revealed), deontological (from Greek *deon*, meaning duty or moral obligation), and utilitarian (produces the greatest good for the greatest number). Kant's categorical imperative states, "Act only according to a maxim by which you can, at the same time, will that it should become a general law." This may be translated as "never adopt a principle of action that you would not be prepared to see everyone else adopt."

The basic stand of many is the belief that it is religious faith that provides the ultimate basis for all standards. That is not so. The difference between the religious and the nonreligious is that the former accepts the moral values prescribed by his faith, while the latter accepts values that are continually questioned and, if necessary, adapted to new circumstances in the light of experience, new knowledge, and rational argument.

To make the right choices, we have to first select the goals and the way of life that is of greatest value to us. Yet most of us have little or no formal ethical training beyond Sunday school. Many of us teach and believe in the wrong ethics. The great Judeo-Christian tradition is individualistic. The Bible, one of the traditional sources of our values, and most of the other sources, are intrinsically inappropriate, or at best undeveloped, as guides to collective and institutional behavior. We have no collective ethic that could be applied to our contemporary world with its global networks, large-scale enterprises, and mass institutions.

A current vogue among ethicists is "value clarification." The assumption is that if you understand the origins of your values and make them clear, harmony will result. There is little evidence that value clarification promotes solutions. It will give us insight, but is only the first step and is no substitute for finding answers.

⨭

"It is the greatest good to the greatest number of people which is the measure of right and wrong." (FB: Bentham used his "hedonic calculus" to total the pleasure and pain of given actions.)

—JEREMY BENTHAM (1748–1832)

Absolute or Relative?

Marcia Angell (1939–) writes in *NEJM,* October 20, 1988: "The fundamental issue is whether ethical issues are relative—to be weighed against competing claims and modified accordingly—or, whether, like scientific standards, they are absolute."

Do all moral questions have at least two sides? That is, are all ethics controversial? Right and wrong do exist, and not all of ethics is controversial. The private morality, as opposed to social morality, is independent of circumstances. It is always wrong to kill, to torture, to humiliate, to steal, to lie, and to break promises. It is always right to be considerate and respectful of others, to be unselfish, charitable, and generous, to take responsibility. Good values are absolute, not what one individual values.

In *Reason and Morals* (Cambridge University Press, 1961), John Wilson said, "To live the good life, we have to make moral choices. Our choices will be based on our approach to the problems which can be moralistic or factualist." The moralist thinks that he knows what is right. He refers to a moral code in judging right or wrong; he looks at people as though they could be entirely good or bad; he is more concerned with what ought to be than what is. The factualist thinks you should do right because it yields a good result. He refers to reality and relative needs; on moral issues he looks for reasons for action and tries to assess the total character and situation of the person. The moralist forbids something because he believes it to be wrong in principle. The factualist forbids an activity only if greater harm would result from allowing it.

There are many aspects to every problem, and no moral principles that apply under all circumstances. There is no way to decide, with certainty, which actions are right or wrong unless you believe in revealed truth. There is no source from which absolute morality could come. That does not exempt us from making moral judgments; it only means that we cannot be sure that we are right.

&

"The achievement of objective rules is a mark of civilization, relativism is a mark of chaos."

—GOETHE (1749–1832)

"Important principles must be inflexible."

—ABRAHAM LINCOLN (1809–1865)

"Morality cannot really exist except in a system of absolutes. It cannot live in relativity where it is just a matter of calculations."

—LESZEK KOLAKOWSKI (1927–2009)

[John Paul II's encyclical, *Veritatis Splendor*] "asserts ... that the morality of an act does not inhere in its context, or its circumstances, or its intentions, or the process by which the individual conscience comes to its decision. Its morality lies simply in the act itself; and certain acts are just wrong, forbidden, anathema, *intrinsece malum* in the delightful Latin phrase, always and everywhere, by anyone and everyone, now and forever."

—ANDREW SULLIVAN (1963–), *TNR*, January 31, 1994

"[Are] ethical standards matters of custom, like table manners[?] Does apartheid offend universal standards of justice, or ... simply represent a South African custom? There must be a core of human rights that we would wish to see honored universally. The force of local custom or law cannot justify abuses of certain fundamental rights, such as the right of self-determination, on which the doctrine of informed consent is based."
—MARCIA ANGELL (1939–), *NEJM*, October 20, 1988

Conflicting Values

Under many systems of government there is a penalty for being honest. Those who suppress a truth that would injure others prove themselves to be part of the human family because they have had to struggle with a conflict of values. The moral rules claim both that honesty is always right, and that one should be loyal to one's fellows in suffering. Liberty and equality, freedom and order, and justice and mercy are often in conflict. The virtuous person is not the one who follows a rule, but the one who understands which rule to follow.

&

"Doing the right thing is easy. Knowing what the right thing is, is more difficult."
—HARRY TRUMAN (1884–1972)

"[N]ot all the supreme values pursued by mankind now or in the past were necessarily compatible with one another. ...[but] it does not follow that ... some must be true and others false. ... We are doomed to choose and every choice may entail an irreparable loss."
—ISAIAH BERLIN (1909-1997), *NYR*, March 17, 1988

"When confronted with a choice between two evils, do not choose."
—DESIDERIUS ERASMUS (1466–1536)

"Wretchedness is the lot of those who do not have the strength to be honorable nor the courage to be dishonorable."
IVAN KLIMA (1931–), *Judge on Trial* (Vintage, 1994)

"There is a certain degree of temptation that will overcome any virtue."
—SAMUEL JOHNSON (1709–1784)

Conventional Morality

Morals should be based on reality, not revelation: a trickle-up value system. We are social beings, living through the eyes of others. Though morality consists in acting in ways that we believe would be endorsed by others, conventional morality is not intrinsically admirable. We must not allow the ideal of rational freedom to mislead us into supposing that there is any moral freedom, or anything of intrinsic value, in the life of conventional morality.

A good case can be made for R. D. Laing's (1927–1989) point of view, as expressed in *The Politics of Experience* (Ballantine Books, 1967): "The family's function is to repress Eros; to induce a false consciousness of security; to deny death by avoiding life; to cut off transcendence; to believe in God, not to experience the Void; to create, in short, one-dimensional man; to promote respect, conformity, obedience; to con children out of play; to induce a fear of failure; to promote a respect for work; to promote a respect for respectability."

EVOLUTION

Adaptation of living things can arise by natural selection, without the need of intelligence. This adaptation can be the product of an algorithmic process.

Man is not necessarily a product of circumstances but of choice.

We have to include in our worldview phenomena that physics and chemistry and other natural sciences expressly leave out: namely life, knowledge, and evolution. The notion of "emergence," however—i.e., that life emerges somehow from "suitably organized" matter—has no comprehensible meaning.

Sociobiology—the study of the biological bases of social behavior—like all evolutionary sciences, is completely at odds with fundamentalist Christianity.

❧

"I cannot look at the universe as the result of blind chance, yet I can see no evidence of beneficent design, or indeed of design of any kind, in the details … .The mystery of the beginning of all things is insoluble by us; and I for one must be content to remain an agnostic."
—CHARLES DARWIN (1809–1882)

"Darwin's central problem is in essence still ours. Can the mindless, purposeless, mechanical process of natural selection fully account for the superb design of living things? Can organized complexity arise from primeval simplicity without the help of a designer or pre-existing mind?"

—DANIEL C. DENNETT (1942–), *Darwin's Dangerous Idea*
(Simon & Schuster, 1996)

"Nothing in biology makes sense except in the light of evolution."

—THEODOSIUS DOBZHANSKY (1900–1975), *American Biology Teacher*,
March 1973

"[To] some nineteenth-century thinkers—Hegel, Marx— ... there were no timeless truths. There was historical development, continuous change; human horizons altered with each new step in the evolutionary ladder."

—ISAIAH BERLIN (1909–1997), *NYR*, March 17, 1988

"The gist of his tale is that technology altered human evolution—and that mankind is unique in thus affecting its own biology through its inventions."

—*The Economist*, review of *Self-Made Man* by Jonathan Kingdom,
March 27, 1993

"Why did Europeans conquer non-European people? Not because of genetic superiority but because of their early exposure to domestic animals, which gave the Europeans immunities to devastating diseases that South American Indians did not have. The presence of domesticated animals happened accidentally."

—JARED DIAMOND (1937–), *Guns, Germs and Steel* (Norton, 1997)

"It is not the strongest species that survives, nor the most intelligent, but the one most responsive to change."

—CHARLES DARWIN (1809–1882)

F

FRIENDSHIP, LOYALTY

There is one good thing to be said about the passage of time. It is the only way you get to be old friends. There just isn't any shortcut to the long run.

How we behave toward each other matters more than what we believe. What happens to us will depend on it; we have to live with the consequences of our behavior.

To accept a gift represents a commitment. This applies even to true gifts that were made with no strings attached.

Loyalty: If any of my friends does anything you do not like, it simply means that you do not understand what he is doing.

Loyalty is not a substitute for any set of consistent ethical and political values.

❧

Byron (1788–1824) dedicated the fourth canto of his poem, "Childe Harold's Pilgrimage," to his great friend John Hobhouse: "To one whom I have known long, and accompanied far, whom I have found wakeful over my sickness and kind in my sorrow, glad in my prosperity and firm in my adversity, true in counsel and trust in peril—to a friend often tried and never found wanting."

"I am wealthy in my friends."

—SHAKESPEARE (1564–1616)

"One must believe in the genuine possibility of a friendship to develop in order for it to come into existence. One acts friendly in order to establish friendship."

—WILLIAM JAMES (1842–1910)

"What qualities would you like most in an individual in your command? First is loyalty, and don't forget it. Without loyalty you are on quicksand. Second is courage. Third is intelligence."

—GENERAL DOUGLAS MACARTHUR (1880–1964)

"Those who mind don't matter, and those who matter don't mind."

—BERNARD BARUCH (1870–1965)

"If you can't get along with me, it's your own fault."

—ALLEN GINSBERG (1926–1997)

"A person who is a stranger to doubt is difficult to have as a friend."

—T. STAPLETON

Said Christopher Robin about friendship: "It's a very comforting sort of thing to have."

—A. A. MILNE (1882–1956)

G

GOVERNMENT

Mundus vult gubernari—the world insists on being governed.

What is best for the individual is not necessarily best for society. Most of our problems arise from a lack of recognition of this fact. How can we combine personal freedom with social ethics and social responsibility? Communism tried to do this but failed miserably.

When routine solutions do not work, you must do something about it. Our routine ways of handling poverty, violence, and moral values obviously do not work. That is why we have to be innovative, progressive, and open-minded.

Thoughts on Government

Questions I ask myself:

- Why do we have such a large budget deficit? Is it due to defense? To Social Security?
- Why do we have a low level of education? We are spending more on it than anybody else.
- Why do we have a higher crime rate than many other countries?
- Why is there such an abuse of social services here?
- Why do people often vote in ways patently contrary to their own material self-interest?

Our federal government is the mechanism by which we tax ourselves to meet collective national needs:

- Government should be limited to national defense, the provision of policy and law, court services, and the protection of individual rights.
- Security from violence is a personal right. The first obligation of the government, of all governments, is securing citizens from violence. A victim of violence should have the right to claim financial damage payments from government for defaulting on its obligation to protect citizens from violent crime.
- The purpose of government is to protect the weak from the strong. Charity has to be available to those who need it. It should be dispensed by the state, not by ethnic or religious groups.
- There is a private sphere that governments may not invade, even for the obvious benefit of those affected.
- We need a government to defend us against corporate America.
- Our government was established to serve the people, not the other way around.

What the West stands for includes democracy, freedom of religion, and the rule of law. I cannot think of any unifying concepts the East stands for.

જી

"Those things that concern an individual alone ought not to be regulated by the state or society but those things that are public can be regulated. The public sphere includes the protection of individuals from violence, the ensuring of public health, and use of taxation to fulfill public services such as education and transportation. ... Individuals have the right to choose how they wish to live, the values that they wish to cherish, even the mistakes that they may freely choose to make, without any interference by society or the state."

—PAUL KURTZ (1925–2012), *Free Inquiry,* Winter 1995/96

"I believe that the sole function of government is to protect life, liberty, and property and anything more than this is usurpation and oppression."

—EZRA TAFT BENSON (1899–1994)

"The function of government is to do good in society."

—DANIEL PATRICK MOYNIHAN (1927–2003)

"The only thing that saves us from bureaucracy is inefficiency. An efficient bureaucracy is the greatest threat to liberty."

—EUGENE MCCARTHY (1916–2005)

"Because something may improve people's lives does not give a government the proper authority to do it."

—JOHN LOCKE (1632–1704), 1690

"Government is not reason, it is not eloquence; it is force. Like fire, it is a dangerous servant and a fearful master."

—GEORGE WASHINGTON (1732–1799)

"The issue today is the same as it has been throughout all history: whether man shall be allowed to govern himself or be ruled by a small elite."

—THOMAS JEFFERSON (1743–1826)

Economic and Political Systems I: Economic Aspects

Industry invests in the present; the government invests in the future.

What are the basic laws of economics? 1) you cannot spend more than you make; 2) you must have reserves to take care of unforeseen events.

The most powerful incentive is for individuals to be able to enjoy the fruits of their labor, to be free to spend and invest their incomes.

You can have a free-market economy without political freedom, but you cannot have political freedom without a free economy. Political freedom without economic health is meaningless. Poor economic systems—not scarcity—create worldwide hunger for millions of people. Powerful nations and empires are destroyed from within not by conquest or assault but by internal economic weakness, by the decay of their social structures and the rotting of their moral fibers.

Prosperity and sound economics are based on the following four principles: 1) political pluralism; 2) constitutional guarantees; 3) private property; and 4) market economy. The "turnpike theorem" is a microeconomics term defining the fastest way of achieving an optimal situation. We should follow a straight turnpike based on these four principles instead of a winding road of half-measures, ill-motivated concessions, delays and ideological errors and prejudices.

According to the Austrian school of economics, value is subjective and cannot be quantified. It is not possible to make a reliable prediction because the outcome is affected by more factors than we can identify. However, we have expectations and we can make assumptions and we should act on them. Instead of making predictions, we should set goals.

The world's dynamic is no longer capitalism v. communism. Now it is open society v. central planning. Ludwig von Mises (1881–1973) criticized centrally planned economies because planners can't know what to produce before they know what people want, and people can't decide what they want until they know the price of things. But prices are only established when people are permitted to own things and exchange them among themselves, rights that do not exist in centrally planned economies.

Following the set blueprint of a planned economy is unresponsive to new information and opportunities. Alternatively, concentrating on processes, rather than imposing some unknown and unknowable collective preference, allows society to evolve and enables individuals to continue to transform themselves. Unpredictability and self-transformation represent desirable human traits on which a policy relying on individual volition can be grounded.

Central banking has also failed to improve on free banking, a further case of the overall failure of central planning. The difference between the two is nothing more than private planning based on economic profit v. bureaucratic planning based on political expediency. Banking should be governed by the rule of law and contract, not by the arbitrary rule of men.

Webster's dictionary says that "capitalism is an economic system in which the means of production, distribution and exchange are privately owned and operated for profit." Its motivation is the desire for private profit. The problem with capitalism is that frequently wealth is not used as an end in itself but as a means of gathering more wealth. The socialist system, seeking equality, vests ownership and control of the means of production and capital in the community as a whole. There the problem is that it does not allow for individual liberty. In his *Autobiography*, philosopher Karl Popper (1902–1994) wrote, "freedom is more important than equality; the attempt to realize equality endangers freedom; and if freedom is lost, there will not even be equality among the unfree." (Library of Living Philosophers Volume XIV © 1974 by Open Court)

The failure of socialism indicates that most people are not inherently good or trusting. Nor has socialism removed its classic objections to capitalism's "inefficiency and waste of ruinous competition." Socialism's aim was that an elite group would oversee the allocation of resources. But the triumph of capitalism has not solved our problems either. It may be the engine of economic progress, and more productive and efficient than socialism, but it also causes uneven distribution of income and greed.

Capitalism may not even have triumphed. What we witnessed in the USSR was the victory of democracy over totalitarianism. Nor did communism go under because of socialist practices. It went under because of economic mismanagement. The managing director of the State Bank of the Soviet Union once said, "In this country there is almost no understanding of the elementary laws of economics. When people in power decided on a project they just told us, 'Get the money for it.' These habits persist." In the United States we don't print money in response to political demands. Instead we borrow it by printing bonds or collect it through taxes that have little regard for the nation's long-term economic health. Politicians do not do what is best for the nation; they do what guarantees their jobs.

We also believed in growth, said Robert H. Nelson in *Forbes* (January 25, 1991), and "that the elimination of poverty and the provision of abundant supplies of goods and services would soon end most ... problems of mankind ... because the basis of past human misbehavior had been the scarcity of resources." But the tremendous material progress that has taken place has not improved our behavior, and the notion of progress has lost its universal luster. Some environmentalists are against it, and against efficiency as well, when it affects their aims. "So," says Nelson, "capitalism needs new moral arguments and spiritual dimensions if it is to endure; efficiency is no longer defense enough."

Does economic growth cause an increase in the income of the rich relative to that of the poor? Not necessarily. Democracy does not protect us against self-serving regulation. Special privileges enforced by government policy have far more to do with the unequal distribution of income than do rates of economic growth. The big danger to a good government is the lobbyists, the organized groups that are held together by their self-interest, who want preferential treatment. They want to control economic access not by the forces of free markets but by nonmarket forces such as licenses, planning boards, and awards of government contracts and tax concessions.

We need laws that will protect our property during our lifetime and after death. Unless property rights are protected, universal voting is or can be a license to redistribute our fortunes. Government does not have the right to appropriate and redistribute the wealth that it did not create. How can it justify estate and inheritance taxes?

What happened to American capitalism is that the financial aspect has overwhelmed the production aspect. If you are constantly seeing everything in terms of maximizing profit, you are not creating a better kind of life. You are constantly undercutting every other norm, whether it is medical care, legal work, or responsible journalism.

Rather than fighting over the size of slices, we should be—and can be—enlarging the pie.

੭ৎ

"Capitalism is the consequent of individual liberty in the economic sphere. We owe to it almost everything that passes under the general name of civilization today."

—H. L. MENCKEN (1880–1956)

"With taxes we build civilization."

—OLIVER WENDELL HOLMES (1841–1935)

"The annual life cycle of federal funding and the short time horizons of political democracies are incongruous when set against the long life cycle of human development and social change."

—*Science*, February 2, 1996

"Economists talk about the profit motive but nothing motivates modern man more than the chance to avoid taxes. We have to tax consumption and decrease taxes on savings. We need a value added tax badly."

—PETER DRUCKER (1909–2005),
Forbes, August 19, 1991

"You don't solve problems, you survive problems."

—THOMAS AQUINAS (1225–1274), according to Peter Drucker

"Corporations are in effect private governments functioning without the consent of the governed. They make decisions on the basis of self-interest rather than the public good, even though they have enormous influence over the public good. They are anti-democratic. They are modeled on the military. People at the bottom need not know why they are doing what they are doing. We need to insist that other norms besides profit apply."

—ROBERT BELLAH (1927–2013) et al., *The Good Society* (Vintage, 1992)

"The federal government provides what many consider to be public goods, such as national defense and the justice system … [but as] S. I. Hayakawa stated in 1981: 'Federal employees are currently operating over 11,000 commercial or industrial activities that the private sector also performs… Since the business of government is not to be in business, I ask myself why?'… It would appear that there is no *economic* justification for the governmental provision of any of these services… [including] education, highways, hospitals and health care … By subsidizing its own enterprises and taxing and regulating its private competitors, it can drive them from the market … privatization of "public" services is more than just a means of cutting the cost of public service provisions, it is a genuine anti-monopoly policy."

—THOMAS J. DILORENZO (1954–),
The Freeman, June 1, 1989

Economic and Political Systems II: Political Aspects

The opposite of communism is not capitalism. It is pluralism—the conscious acceptance of differences between individuals and groups in a society. The real division of the twentieth century between countries has been between people who live under the aegis of the single truth, the single rule that explains everything and gives things meaning, and those who inhabit nations that acknowledge many truths and many necessities.

The important divisions in outlook between different people are not those between idealism and materialism, fascism and democracy, socialism and capitalism, but between the relative preferences of the community and the individual.

The essence of totalitarianism, whether fascist or communist, is governance by terror. A man who has no paranoia in a totalitarian state is not a healthy man.

In a democracy, the government is responsible to the electorate: it is a system for transforming society by consent. The transfer of power is anchored in public expectation, and the government is responsive to the public will. Italian political scientist Carlo Pelanda (1951–) (www.carlopelanda.com) described democracy as "at bottom an ethical system in which the citizens discipline themselves on the principle that it is better to decide things by the right means than to get their own way."

Though democracy, as the rule of the majority, may not necessarily be a concept of a just society, it is beyond doubt the most desirable form of government. It extends and protects the rights of the opposition, and it has evolved so that minorities have representation in government. But the system by which the government is empowered has to be designed to limit the rule of the majority. The majority is not necessarily right. People's opinions may be influenced by personal motives or seeking political gain, and they may be irresponsible, careless, or misinformed.

According to Jacques Barzun (1907–2012) in his Carnegie Council Morgenthau Lecture (1986), democracy "calls for three difficult things: expressing the popular will, ensuring equality and by means of both, distributing a variety of freedoms. These purposes imply machinery. How, for example, is the popular will ascertained?"

And how is equality ensured? Through taxation to equalize income? Is it "equal" to reward talent with higher pay? Does, as Barzun asks, "merit violate democratic equality because merit is not earned, it is as it were unmerited?"

☙

"The danger that threatens us is the totalitarian empire. Khomeini, Mao, Stalin—[were] they left or right? Totalitarian vision is neither left nor right and within its empire both will perish. ... This is why the stubborn struggle between left and right seems to me obsolete."
—MILAN KUNDERA (1929–), *NYT*, May 18, 1985

"Ur-Fascism," by Umberto Eco (1932–2016) appeared in the *The New York Review of Books* on June 22, 1995. Below, in abbreviated form, is his list of, as he said, "features that are typical of what I like to call Ur-Fascism, or Eternal Fascism."

1) *Cult of tradition.* The culture of syncretism (a combination of different forms of belief or practice). Each message has a sliver of wisdom. Combination must tolerate contradictions. As a consequence there can be no advancement of learning. Truth has already been spelled out once and for all.

2) *Rejection of modernism.* Rejection of Enlightenment, the Age of Reason. It is irrationalism.

3) *Action for action's sake.* Action, being beautiful in itself, must be taken without any previous reflection.

4) *Disagreement is treason.* It can be a way to improve knowledge. It is not treason.

5) Exploiting and exacerbating the natural *fear of differences.* Racism.

6) *Appeal to a frustrated middle class* suffering from an economic crisis and frightened by pressure of lower social groups.

7) *Obsession with a plot.* The only privilege is to be born in the same country. The only ones who can provide an identity to the nation are its enemies.

8) *Humiliation* by the ostentatious wealth of its enemies.

9) There is no struggle for life, but, rather, *life is lived for struggle.* Pacifism is trafficking with the enemy. It is bad because life is permanent warfare.

10) *Elitism* is a typical aspect of any reactionary ideology. Aristocratic and militaristic elitism implies contempt for the weak.

11) Ur-Fascists crave *heroic death.* They are impatient to die and in their impatience often send other people to death.

12) They transfer their will to power to sexual matters. *Machismo* implies disdain for women and intolerance of nonstandard sexual practices such as chastity or homosexuality. Weapons become an ersatz phallic exercise.

13) People do not act by following the decisions of the majority but permit a leader to be their interpreter. Fascism is always *against "rotten" parliamentary governments.*

14) Ur-Fascists speak in *Newspeak* using an impoverished vocabulary and elementary syntax.

Ethics of a Nation I: Social Morality

Eighteenth-century thinker Adam Smith's idea that the general good resulted from individuals pursuing their own well-being required them to behave "rationally." The logic of social organization—not of individual self-interest—is what requires an ethic of selfless behavior.

In defense of the Constitution: religious fundamentalists believe that traditional religion is necessary to morality and that religious morality is necessary to citizenship and culture. Our founding fathers did not believe this or were uncertain. That is why we have the *separation* of church from state.

"The strength or weakness of a society depends more on the level of its spiritual life than on its level of industrialization," said Alexander Solzhenitsyn (1918–2008) in *National Review* (September 23, 1991). Human freedom includes a voluntary self-restraint in favor of others. Our obligation must always exceed the freedom that is granted to us. He reminds us of the universal values underpinning all societies and draws attention to standards that need to be striven for, if not attained.

Much of the morality of the man in the street is based on a "catch-22" proposition. The notion is that we should refuse to help the Mexicans (or the handicapped or underprivileged) to overcome their problems because they have them in the first place. This is not only mean-spirited. It also goes against all the evidence that indicates that prosperity is what generates concern for property rights, human rights, and the environment.

◈

"States that purvey moral claims usually do so only in order to justify or to conceal political self-interest."

—Christoph Frei, *TNR*, June 4, 2001

Ethics of a Nation II: Statistical Morality

Statistics apply to groups, not to individuals.

Dealing with ethical problems in the abstract seems pointless. We cannot deal with issues until we deal with our own biases. We all have feelings, judgments, and values that either magnify or blind us to ethical problems. Jean-Paul Sartre (1905–1980) once said the greatest sin is to turn what is concrete into an abstraction. It is easy to forget, for instance, that living flesh and dead bodies are behind every casualty accounting. It is particularly easy when the air is clogged with stately phrases like "national honor," "measured responses," and "massive retaliation." "Nuclear deterrence" really means that the world is held together by the threat that if millions of people on one side are killed, millions on the other side will also die. To grasp what this means in human terms, one should concentrate on a single death, a single burned body, a single disfigured face.

The thesis that we must limit society's support of more medical care, or make choices as to which medical conditions merit support, has no merit. Life has to be saved irrespective of cost. Who can recommend that an arbitrary cutoff weight of 500 gm should be made, below which no attempt will be made to save premature babies—those weighing 499 gm?

Regulation of a dangerous industry depends on the stance taken toward the valuation of the individual or society. It leads to the establishment of benefit/risk ratios and the assignment of an arbitrary price to a human life. U.S. agencies now have to prove that the benefit of saving lives from cancer induced by a chemical exceeds, in dollar amounts, the cost to the industry of reducing or removing the hazard.

There is no absolute ethical judgment for or against nuclear weapons; rather, the ethics lie in the way the issues are approached and the choices made.

❧

In *Science* (May 5, 1989), Daniel E. Koshland, Jr. (1920–1987) said, "Statistical morality is the precept that a given course of action that may cause some harm to individuals now [is 'acceptable' because it] will result in greater benefit to more individuals in the future." Melvin Krasner responded (in *Science,* July 14, 1989) that this precept "is in dramatic conflict with notions of personal freedom ... and with basic philosophical principles about interpersonal transfers of utility."

"Proposals of seemingly lesser evils to avoid greater ones almost never strike the intended marks."
　　　　　—WILLIAM M. KUNSTLER (1919–1995), *NYT,* August 14, 1989

In "The Poverty of Epidemiology," Petr Skrabanek (1940–1994) wondered "whether epidemiology, in the absence of epidemics, is not a misnomer for scaremongering made respectable by the use of sophisticated statistical methods ... any combination of 'exposure' and disease ... is fair game for calculating relative risks, odds ratios, or proportional hazards." *PBM,* Winter 1992

Freedoms and Human Rights

The basic human freedoms are: government by freely elected representatives; the rule of law; limits on the power of the state; human rights for all; free speech; equal justice; religious tolerance.

Human rights include the right to health and education as well as the right to vote.

Every citizen's freedom ultimately rests upon the guarantee of freedom to all citizens, no matter how small the subgroup to which they belong. The protection of individual rights is a precondition of justice.

The value of liberty is self-evident. It need not be justified by pragmatic arguments. The opportunity to set one's own direction rather than being subject to the will of even a benevolent other is what separates adult from child, free person from slave. Webster's describes freedom as the ability to act and make choices without "necessity, coercion or restraint."

The basic difference between a free and a controlled society: one uses incentives to encourage certain kinds of independent action; the other uses penalties to inhibit them.

One does not suppress false ideas. They too are allowed a forum; they simply need to be countered with argument.

Since no opinion, however odious, can inflict harm, it follows that no one has the right to suppress any opinion. The expression of animosity is not harm. When Smith causes Jones to hate you, you have not been harmed. Harm begins when Jones attacks you. Words are held responsible for harmful acts only when they overwhelm the listener's power of reason, as in shouting "Fire!" in a crowded theater.

We are all for freedom of speech when it deals with the subjects about which we have no firm convictions. In the 1943 compulsory flag salute case, Supreme Court Justice Robert Jackson (1892–1954) wrote: "Freedom to differ is not limited to things that do not matter much. That would be a mere shadow of freedom. The test of its substance is the right to differ as to the things that touch the heart of the existing order."

Two hundred years ago, Edmund Burke (1729–1797) blasted the supporters of the French Revolution for assuming the existence of a universal set of human rights. He argued for what we now call "cultural relativism"—a citizen could understand his "rights" only in relation to his culture. The form of a country's government should be founded on its particular "circumstances and habits."

Tom Paine's (1737–1809) famous reply rejected Burke's appeal to cultural differences: the rights of man were universal and the only legitimate form of government was one that secured those rights.

Serious restrictions on liberty cannot rest solely on appeals to tradition, even when backed by majority approval. There is no evidence that violations of the majority's moral norms such as polygamy threaten the existence of society.

જ

"This institution will be based on the illimitable freedom of the human mind. For here, we are not afraid to follow truth where it may lead, nor to tolerate error so long as reason is free to combat it."
>   —THOMAS JEFFERSON (1743–1826), when establishing the
>   University of Virginia in 1819

"Complete freedom and complete equality are not compatible.
The Bolsheviks brought up the motto of the French Revolution *ad absurdum.*"
>   —FELIX SOMARY (1881–1956)

"The struggle of man against power is the struggle of memory against forgetting."
>   —MILAN KUNDERA (1929–)

"He alone is worthy of life and freedom who each day does battle for them anew."

—GOETHE (1749–1832), *Faust*

"If liberty is abandoned, you will have neither liberty nor bread."

—SIDNEY HOOK (1902–1989)

Health Care

There is nothing wrong with a system that offers everyone employment, food, education, and health care. Public health is the responsibility of the government. The best available medical help is the birthright of every human being irrespective of his or her financial ability to pay for it. We need state medical service.

The Swiss Constitution says a nation's strength can be measured by the welfare of its weak.

Medical needs should be addressed irrespective of cause—smokers should have equal access to bypass as nonsmokers. There should be no punitive rules against self-inflicted injury.

The best thing a nation has to offer is government provision for personal needs, from bathing to feeding, for everybody unable do them on their own, bringing relief from anxiety or even anguish and renewed security in old age.

A free market means that most doctors, laboratories, and radiological services are working as limited companies and competing for business. The United States operates on the assumption that this for-profit, competitive model of medicine will bring down the cost of medical service by forcing the providers of health care to be more economically efficient. There is no evidence in favor of this proposition.

If you agree that the provision of health and medical services is one of the basic human rights, we have to decide whether the profit motive should play a part. Making money and serving patients are fundamentally at odds. Health care should be carried out for its own sake.

એ

"Protecting the health of ordinary people during times of conflict is not an option but the inescapable duty of any nation that considers itself to have any truly meaningful role in world affairs."
                            —*The Lancet*, Editorial, April 13, 2002

"What is the greatest political danger to the medical profession? To be a field of knowledge dominated by economical and not communitarian interests."
                —JUAN CARLOS TEALDI (1951–), *The Lancet*, December 2, 2000

Immigration

It is fundamentally wrong to have quotas, as it nullifies the equality of opportunity.

Immigrants bring with them a demand for goods and services that requires more production and more new jobs.

We cannot be happy if we put people in prisons. Freedom of movement is one of the basic rights of man. A prison is a place one cannot voluntarily enter or leave. Immigration and emigration restrictions make prisons out of states.

ॐ

"Self-determination is clearly flawed as a principle for action. Its central premise is that peoples of different faiths and ethnic compositions cannot live together in harmony. It is a principle based on ... intolerance. It is ... reactionary, and prone to violence, ... inviting majorities to be intransigent, and leads to atomization of human societies. It is also a contradiction of the very principles on which the United States was founded and has prospered."
—RONALD STEEL (1935–), *TNR*, January 21, 1991

"[Immigrants] supposedly take jobs away from 'real Americans,' or women, who take them away from men. In fact, the influx of those two groups into the labor market has not been accompanied by an increase in unemployment, suggesting that individuals create jobs as well as occupy them."
—DANIEL E. KOSHLAND, JR. (1920–1987), *Science*, February 19, 1988

Law and Justice

Laws are quite distinct from ethics. Ethics are concerned with morality, with what is good and what is right. Laws are rules prescribed by those in authority to make society governable.

Our laws should be based on ethical norms on which all men can agree and not only on revelations. This is the basic reason why separation of church and state is so important.

Even when we have laws that are widely accepted, such as those that comprise the U.S. Constitution, questions arise about the interpretation of words and phrases, who should do the interpreting and so on. Thomas Jefferson put the issue in the form of a question: Does the earth belong to the living or the dead? We have to do what appears right and appropriate now, whether or not it is mentioned in the Constitution.

An outcome-oriented concept of justice is insensitive to process (the means of getting there). If all that matters is the destination, the route taken to it is irrelevant.

Justice cannot be the realization of a master design because there is no general agreement or acceptance of such a design. There is no agreement about what is just. Is it just that some people are born with more talents than others? Is it just that some people are so much more successful than others?

Justice's role should be to enhance choices and to secure fair processes rather than particular outcomes for individuals and communities.

The business of the lawyer and the judge is not justice but the law.

When it comes to wartime justice, obedience to orders is no excuse for criminality. A superior can be found guilty for failing to prevent what he could have prevented. The Nuremberg and Tokyo trials sustain these arguments.

❧

"The only positive laws we have are: the dignity of man and the necessity for order."

—REINHOLD NIEBUHR (1892–1971)

"A good end cannot sanctify evil means, nor must we ever do evil that good may come of it."

—WILLIAM PENN (1644–1718)

"There is as much injustice in the equal treatment of unequal cases as there is in the unequal treatment of equal cases."

—ARISTOTLE (384–322 BCE), *Nichomachean Ethics*

"We are under the Constitution, but the Constitution is what the judges say it is."

—CHARLES EVANS HUGHES (1862–1948), Chief Justice,
U.S. Supreme Court

Becoming a lawyer meant joining a helping profession—one which dealt with the problems of people ... [but] lawyers and businessmen alike have gradually come to accept that the client is best able to judge what he needs done and the lawyer must be ready to do whatever the client asks. In acceding to this, the lawyer... deprives the client of the one thing the client is most entitled to have—the best advice the lawyer can give as to whether what the client wants done should really be done. ... Elihu Root's words are worth recalling: 'About half the practice of a decent lawyer consists in telling would-be clients that they are damn fools and should stop.'"

—SOL M. LINOWITZ (1913–2005), *Cosmos Journal 1995,* Cosmos Club,
Washington, D.C.

Nationalism, Patriotism

Nationalism is relentless pride in the accident of birth. Our philosophy and beliefs should not be affected by the accident of birth.

Under nationalism, law reigns only within a sovereignty; internationally, and nationally between civil factions contending sovereignty, anarchy reigns.

Nationalism is based on two things: 1) taking credit for somebody else's achievements and 2) using single-attribute designations to legitimize hate, envy, fear, and feelings of inferiority to rationalize violent behavior. Limiting victims' identities to one attribute denies their full humanity: he is no longer a man, a father, a woodcarver, a farmer, but a bourgeois. She is no longer a woman, a daughter, a lover of poetry, but a Marxist.

Nationalism should be thought of as cultural nationalism only, based on the idea that one's humanity finds its best expression in one's particular culture. Sir William Osler's (1840–1919) example: "In the continual remembrance of a glorious past, individuals and nations find their noblest inspiration."

There is room for different cultures and no need for rivalry among them. How to deal with political nationalism, the theory of superiority, and hatred toward the Other is the problem. Even when it exalts itself in the name and cause of culture, nationalism is indissolubly bound up with racism. It cannot produce or promote culture, of which individual freedom is the only creative source.

Patriotism is to an ideal, not a piece of geography. Need does not constitute a claim.

I know of no statement more immoral than the patriotic attitude expressed in "my country, right or wrong."

৵

"Patriotism and nationalism became the main driving forces of war in 19th-century Europe. War became everyone's business. Poets glorified it. Priests and pastors blessed the weapons."

—Anatol Rapoport (1911–2007), *Queen's Quarterly*, Spring 1996

"Patriotism is the last refuge of a scoundrel."

—Samuel Johnson (1709–1784)

"The worth of a state, in the long run, is the worth of the individuals composing it."

—John Stuart Mill (1806–1873)

"A nation is a group of people united by a mistaken view about the past and a hatred of their neighbors."

—Ernest Renan (1823–1892)

"The idea of a God-chosen nation ... is echoed in a secularized form in countless nationalistic trends."

—Zdeněk Pinc (1945–)

"Religion and patriotism until recently were the chief moral influences. They stood for strife, bloodshed and intolerance. They are not the sole sources of discord but they have hitherto been the chief, and are most deplorable when the forces combine, as in Islam today."

—G. A. Wells (1926–2013), *Belief and Make-Believe*
© 1992 by Open Court

"Power tends to confuse itself with virtue and a great nation is peculiarly susceptible to the idea that its power is a sign of God's favor. ... The arrogance of power [is] a psychological need that nations seem to have in order to prove that they are bigger, better, or stronger than other nations."

—William Fulbright (1905–1995), *The Arrogance of Power*
(Random House, 1966)

"Nationalism can even divorce from all community of brotherhood and goodwill fellow men who simply happen to live on the other side of the river."
—Barbara Ward (1914–1981), *Nationalism and Ideology*
(Norton, 1966)

"Patriotism cannot be our final spiritual shelter; my refuge is humanity. I will not buy glass for the price of diamonds, and I will never allow patriotism to triumph over humanity as long as I live."
—Rabindranath Tagore (1861–1941), Letter to a friend, 1908

Political Parties and Positions

Politics is not about expediency but about purpose. It is here to advance the common good and should be rooted in morality and not in self-interest.

The two-word summaries of political parties' platforms: Conservative (Republican)—business and ambition; Labor (Democrat)—compassion and justice.

Many Republicans take Herbert Hoover's view that the sole function of government is to bring about a condition of affairs favorable to private enterprise. Roosevelt Democrats argue that the government also has the obligation to prevent the starvation or the dire want of its citizens.

The three main components of conservatism are anticommunism, racism, and fear of social disintegration.

For them, personal rights and liberties and property rights have dominance over social improvement objectives. Medical care and medical insurance should be personal matters and the individual, not the employer, should be responsible for their provision. It is not known what is best—Western medicine, holistic medicine, Christian Science, or acupuncture. Let the user decide and pay for it. Do not force 100 percent of the people to take care of the general requirements of 5 percent—who may be handicapped, underprivileged, unlucky, etc.

The Moral Right, while extolling its religion-based code of conduct, overlooks one aspect of the Christian ethic—its imperative to love.

The liberalism of the founding fathers, a liberalism that is expressed in the Bill of Rights, is based on freedom of expression, association, and religion, and civil equality. The cornerstone of New Deal liberalism posits that the state play a role in guaranteeing the basic welfare of all citizens and in protecting employees from exploitation by powerful corporations.

The distinction between what is public and what is private is critical to the understanding of liberalism. Liberals are interested in the conditions that promote progress. Liberal doctrine proclaims that individual rights are paramount. Coercion implies an unjustified claim of knowledge, even certainty. People should be left to make their own choices. This is the case for liberalism.

Liberal beliefs include abortion, gay rights, women in the military, legalizing marijuana, legalizing prostitution, opposition to capital punishment, gun control, opposition to school prayer, and opposition to the Vietnam, Iraq, and Afghanistan wars.

Liberalism champions ideas that are as fundamental to progress of the right as of the left: 1) individual liberty; 2) human equality; 3) religious tolerance; 4) inquiry based on the free exercise of human reason. Controversies between the left and the right take place in large measure within this liberal framework.

The problem of liberals: they are open to new analyses and yet reluctant to engage in genuinely radical action.

According to William F. Buckley, Jr. (1925-2008), "The problem with liberals was not so much that their beliefs were wrong, but that they lacked any real beliefs at all." (FB: This may be the only proper attitude when the ultimate truth is not known.)

Samuel Gompers (1850–1924) was co-founder and first president of the American Federation of Labor. From one of his speeches: "What does labor want? We want more schoolhouses and less jails, more books and less guns, more learning and less vice, more leisure and less greed, more justice and less revenge. We want more opportunities to cultivate our better nature."

೨

"Politics is the justice of life but not its essence—playing the game is essential as long as it does not become an end in itself."
—Derrick Silove, *The Lancet,* July 22, 2000

"Politics does not create new realities. It can only take advantage of those that exist, suppressing some parts and intensifying others. Human nature, not politics, spins the thread of history."
—I. L. Peretz (1852–1915), in *The I .L. Peretz Reader*
(Yale University Press, 2002)

"I think that's the difficulty in politics. You are always bound to lose supporters once you take a stand on an issue."
—JOHN FITZGERALD KENNEDY (1917–1963), 1951

"Madness is rare in individuals but in groups, parties, nations and epochs, it is the rule."
—FRIEDRICH NIETZSCHE (1844–1900)

"The behavior of groups is strikingly immature … they are, from a psychological standpoint, less than the sum of their parts."
—M. SCOTT PECK (1936–2005), *People of the Lie*
(Simon & Schuster, 1998)

"'Is there one single maxim that could ruin a country?' Confucius replied: 'Mere words could not achieve this. There is a saying, however: "The only pleasure of being a prince is never to have to suffer contradiction." If you are right and no one contradicts you, that's fine. But if you are wrong and no one contradicts you—is this not a case of one single maxim that could ruin a country?'"
—CONFUCIUS (551–479 BCE), *Analects,* tr. Simon Leys (Norton, 1997)

Waging War

Tragedy is a struggle to the death when both sides are right.

Why do we have wars? Why do we have terrorism? Because a group of people believe with absolute certainty that truth has been revealed to them. The revealed truth may be a religion, the teaching of Marx or Lenin, or any other doctrine.

Criminality and violence are learned, not genetic. Warfare is cultural, not biological.

You cannot prevent violence or terrorism by starting a war. By starting a war, one just legalizes murder.

The army and those in power try to change us so that we follow orders without questioning, and also try to break the innate inhibition most people have against killing.

Can war ever be morally justifiable? It cannot. If you prepare for war, you train human beings to kill other human beings.

No problem has ever been solved by waging war. We must try to overcome such medieval or juvenile concepts as that patriotic men will defend their country with their lives. Soldiers rarely know or understand why a war is being waged.

All agree that modern weaponry must be used in a way that does no harm to civilian populations. This is impossible. Poison gas, infectious microorganisms, radiation, and bombing cannot be used in such a way.

I see that many individuals are against the use of chemical and biological weapons in war. It is apparently okay to bomb civilian populations. But murder is murder whether committed by chemical, biological, or conventional weapons. We are in great danger that our planet will be ruled by a single well-armed superpower. We are well on the way. We can prevent it only if we all agree to solve our problems peacefully and totally and universally.

の

"There is a legitimate use of force, but any ethics requires that it be legitimated. Force alone cannot legitimate its use. That seems to me to be almost a foundation thought of ethics."

—BERNARD WILLIAMS (1929-2003), *The Center Magazine,*
November/December 1983

H

HAPPINESS, CONTENTMENT

Our mission is not to make people happy but to allow them to be themselves.

Our task is to perceive and care, not to observe and analyze.

To be happy we must be alive to all of the dimensions of life: to the arts that help us to understand what we have and teach us to acquire an appreciation of it, to the sciences that tell us how things and beings work and how they got that way, and to ethics that try to find out how things ought to be and how human beings ought to behave.

Our problem is our difficulty in deciding what is important, what is worthwhile, what will give us satisfaction and contentment and what will not. Instead of relying on ourselves and the wise men of the past and the present, we listen and try to imitate those who are in positions of power and authority.

Plato (427–347 BCE) argued that happiness and satisfaction cannot be attained by living the life of pleasure. They can only be achieved by fulfilling one's purpose and by leading a life of virtue. Virtue is the action that flows from knowledge. Indeed, virtue *is* knowledge.

Most people try to induce a state of contentment by pointing out how fortunate they are by being healthier or richer than their less fortunate brethren. This does not work. There are only three ways to induce contentment: 1) by completely concentrating on a task that is within one's realm of competence and is of interest to us; 2) by sex with an understanding and caring partner; and 3) by certain drugs. Each of these methods has its limitations.

Happiness is like coke fuel—something you get as a by-product in the process of making something else.

We must not use our past experiences and misfortunes to excuse our unhappiness and failure. It is the here and now that is important, not the psychological impediments we experienced in the past.

Four gates to happiness and success:
1) Do not worry about things you cannot avoid. Use them to enrich your life.
2) All those who are born must die. Let this insight awaken you to life's preciousness and fragility.
3) All those who are alive know pain and suffering. Use this knowledge to show you the way to wisdom.
4) You cannot control your destiny by proper attitude or correct behavior, but you have a choice in how to respond to adversity and failure.

Harmony and contentment cannot be found until working and spending is displaced as the first focus of daily life. It is necessary to overcome consumerism.

Perhaps happiness is not a goal but a road. Perhaps pursuit of happiness is that happiness.

ॐ

"If I can make somebody happy, I have achieved a mighty purpose."
                                    —ARNOLD GLASOW (1905–1988)

"I may surely be contented without the praise of perfection which, if I could obtain it, in this gloom of solitude, what would it avail me? I have protracted my work till most of those whom I wished to please have sunk into the grave, and success and miscarriage are empty sounds. I therefore dismiss it with frigid tranquility, having little to fear or hope from censure or from praise."
                    —SAMUEL JOHNSON (1709–1784), end of his preface to
                                    Dictionary of the English Language

"[Quennell] notes that Samuel Johnson and Turgenev both saw happiness as something that is elusive in the present, something that is accessible only through memory or hope; he goes on to show that many writers, from Byron to Proust, have located happiness in the nostalgic past of their schooldays or childhood."
                    MICHIKO KAKUTANI (1955–), reviewing *The Pursuit of Happiness*
                                    by Peter Quennell, *NYT*, December 31, 1988

"When it comes to saying in what happiness consists, opinions differ … and often the same person actually changes his opinion. When he falls ill he says it is his health and when he is hard up he says that it is money."
                                    —ARISTOTLE (384–322 BCE)

"Does happiness result from ignorance or from knowledge?"
                                    —VOLTAIRE (1694–1778)

"To avoid thinking is the secret of a happy life."
                                    —DESIDERIUS ERASMUS (1466–1536)

"Too much of a good thing can be wonderful."

—MAE WEST (1893–1980)

"When we are happy we are always good but when we are good we are not always happy."

—OSCAR WILDE (1854–1900)

HEREDITY, GENES

We are what we are not only because of our genes but also because of what we believe, what we expect, and what we do. We need and would benefit from a clearer understanding of all the influences that affect our desires and actions: Why *do* we do what we do?

The important thing is not what kind of genes you get but what you do with them.

Words and experience can influence biochemical processes as well as vice versa.

Most of an individual's genes are sequestered in the nuclei of his or her cells and are derived in equal parts from both the mother and the father. In contrast, all the mitochondria in our cells are inherited from our mothers, and therefore contain DNA from the mother only. Mitochondria are filaments or rods located in the cell protoplasm outside the nucleus of the cell. They are concerned with cellular respiration, protein synthesis, and lipid metabolism. Mitochondrial DNA analysis offers the most direct opportunity to trace ancestral lineage. It obviates the need to pick out which parent donated which gene sequences and simplifies lineage determination to genetic inheritance from just one parent—the mother—to the next generation.

The identification of genes reveals their roles in causing hereditary diseases and indicates ways toward treatment. While most diseases are not hereditary, the risk factors lending predisposition to them are.

આ

The nominator of *The Lancet*'s prizewinning 2003 Paper of the Year described it as "of utmost importance. … The general biological lesson is that the overwhelming source of human genetic variation is between individuals and not between ethnic groups." Noah Rosenberg and colleagues' "Genetic Structure of Human Populations" appeared in *Science,* December 20, 2002. The award was announced in *The Lancet,* December 20–27, 2003.

"Where I was born and where and how I have lived is unimportant. It is what I have done with where I have been that should be of interest."
—GEORGIA O'KEEFFE (1887–1986)

HOMOSEXUALITY

For a small minority of people, homosexuality is an involuntary condition that can be neither denied nor permanently repressed without serious consequences.

The recognition by the state, church, and society that homosexuality is an inherent and natural condition establishes a very important point. It indicates that the primary function of sexuality is not procreation. Thus sex, whether hetero or homo, appears to be a natural drive that requires fulfillment for its own sake.

Sexual orientation is a private matter. Conduct and behavior make it acceptable or unacceptable.

Erich Fromm (1900–1980) said, "The deepest need of man is the need to overcome his separateness, to leave the prison of his aloneness." The solution, he suggests, is the achievement of fusion with another person in a loving relationship. It makes little difference if that other person is of the same sex.

A condition that is innate (literally *innatus* or "inborn") is morally neutral, since anything involuntary could not be moral or immoral; it simply exists, like cases of homosexuality.

ॐ

"There is nothing more fruitless than wanting to be something other than I am by nature."

—TCHAIKOVSKY (1840–1893)

"Fancy not anything in the world—any more—to be of any weight and moment but this: to do that which your own nature requires."

—MARCUS AURELIUS (121–180)

ON BEING HUMAN

What makes a human being a human? It is the unique ability to have ideas, create abstract concepts, and take an interest in religion, philosophy, art, and science.

One of the attributes of being human is having compassion. This means that you are concerned about people, even if you are not related to them and even if they do not look like you or come from your country.

For humans, consciousness has so developed it has become conscience: we wonder what the right thing to do is. Life appears to us as a challenge to create what ought to be from what is.

Conscience, compassion, and humor are the qualities that make us human. We must not sacrifice them to politics.

A basic human need: to receive recognition for the good things one has done.

❧

"To be human is to be able to help others, not for one's own sake, but for the sake of others."
—Theodore Zeldin (1933–), *An Intimate History of Humanity*
(Harper Perennial, 1995)

"Man is the product of what he has done and of what has been done to him."

—Louis Chedid, MD

"Man is something to be surpassed. What have you done to surpass him?"

—Friedrich Nietzsche (1844–1900)

I

INTELLIGENCE, INFORMATION, KNOWLEDGE, WISDOM

Intelligence: Human and Artificial

Is intelligence a single, general dimension along which individuals vary, or is it a range of many different abilities?

Intelligence should never be confused with wisdom.

Intelligence-test developer Alfred Binet's (1857–1911) summary of the nature of intelligence: the ability to understand directions, to maintain a mental set, and to apply self-criticism.

There are two attributes that make certain behavior appear intelligent. First, the behavior appears reasonably appropriate to the situation. Second, it is not totally predictable.

According to developmental expert Howard Gardner (1943–) in *Frames of Mind: The Theory of Multiple Intelligences* (Basic Books, 2001), every child, every person, has various forms of intelligence that will begin to show up in response to the way we seek them out. An intelligence is the ability to solve problems, or to create products, that are valued within one or more cultural settings. The SAT exams tap only two of the seven kinds of intelligence that Gardner describes.

Marvin Minsky (1927–2016), a pioneer in artificial intelligence, said to be intelligent, a machine must 1) learn from experience; 2) know how to correct its own mistakes; and 3) be able to view a problem in more than one way. Machines cannot define a problem. They lack creativity.

Computers have no common sense. They can handle only facts and truth, but facts and truth are only good in mathematics and that is an artificial system. There are very few things that are always true. Mathematical logic cannot handle exceptions. Common sense does. Logic cannot say which things are most important in a given framework.

Computers solve problems in ways that are not suggestive of human intelligence. How computers work seems to have no real relevance to how the mind works, any more than a wheel shows how people walk.

"People often think of intelligence as quickness of thought or propensity for flashes of insight. But ... those qualities may not be at the root of it. Instead, a key ingredient of intelligence may be the ability to juggle lots of possibilities in the mind. ... Language comprehension is important but appears to be an independent factor."

—INGRID WICKELGREN, *Science,* March 14, 1997

"The test of a first-rate intelligence is the ability to hold two opposed ideas in the mind at the same time, and still retain the ability to function."

—F. SCOTT FITZGERALD (1896–1940), *The Crack-Up,* 1945 (New Directions, 1993)

"It is not the intelligence you have; it is what you do with it."

—THOMAS BERGER, 1971

"The computer is not capable of initiating improvement by itself. You can't innovate by computer."

—MILTON FRIEDMAN (1912–2006), *Forbes,* December 12, 1988

Information

The Internet is the widest storehouse of information the world has ever had. But there are differences among information, knowledge, and wisdom. Information is the raw material of knowledge. Having knowledge gives one the ability to use information to answer questions, and wisdom is the ability to ask the important questions. So what makes all the difference is not the information one has at one's disposal, but the judgment in using it.

Information technology and the Internet are inventions that permit us to do old things in new ways, so we have to invent things that never existed. The incredible means of communication that science and technology have given us can and should be used to promote the unity of mankind. This is the only way to avoid the dangers of the atomic age. At the same time, we must avoid becoming a nation of specialists. Specialism is a state of mind that favors technical training at the expense of liberal culture and stops communication between scholar and scholar, between scholar and layman, and between man and man.

Information is cybernetic, that is, common to living organisms and machines. But who has seen an enlightened machine?

Information overload: 90 percent of the written material most of us see is worthless because it either repeats what we already know or is irrelevant.

಄

"Information, in its new scientific sense, is utterly divorced from meaning. Chaotic systems, and strings of random numbers, altogether meaningless, are dense with information."
—JAMES GLEICK (1954–) on Claude Shannon, *NYT*, December 30, 2001

"What to do with too much information is the great riddle of our time. ... That is what the modern search is for: where to go next. ...it has become impossible for traditions about how to live to be handed down to the next generation."

—THEODORE ZELDIN (1933–), *An Intimate History of Humanity* (Harper Perennial, 1995)

Knowledge

Since knowledge and wisdom are different, what it all comes down to is converting knowledge into wisdom and then into vision. As the Greek poet Philostratus (170–250) wrote: "For the gods perceive things in the future, ordinary people things in the present, but the wise perceive things about to happen."

What is it that is important to know? Is it really important to know what pi is unless you are a mathematician? Most people who seek an explanation for their problems assume the reason is a lack of knowledge, a void where there should be facts. It may be that lack of knowledge is not the problem at all, but rather that people know a lot of "facts" that simply are not factual. The problem is not the lack of information but too much disinformation.

More knowledge of the world around us and of ourselves is needed for its own sake. Some of the new knowledge will be beneficial, and some will be potentially dangerous.

ॐ

"Knowledge must be an end in itself. Knowledge must be integrated with other first principles, among them free inquiry, intellectual honesty, trust in rationality, and the moral obligation of conveying the results of research to others. Institutions of learning must overcome an obsession with relevance and immediacy."

—Jaroslav Pelikan (1923–2006), *The Idea of the University: A Reexamination* (Yale University Press, 1992)

"All knowledge is vain and erroneous excepting that brought into the world by sense perception, the mother of all certainty."

—Leonardo da Vinci (1452–1519)

"Human knowledge is the result of our own ordering of sense experience, which by itself would be unintelligible. We impose *a priori* categories upon experience, e.g. categories of space, time and relation. Without them there could be no understanding of our experience and there can be no knowledge of that which is beyond our experience."

—Immanuel Kant (1724–1804)

"To know that we know what we know, and that we do not know what we do not know, that is true knowledge."

—Confucius (551–479 BCE), *Analects*, tr. Simon Leys (Norton, 1997)

Wisdom

Wisdom is knowledge in practice. Knowledge of the law of gravity does not free us from gravity but makes it easier for us to use it to our advantage.

Wisdom's most basic definition is avoiding the unnecessary.

The foundation of wisdom is that there is no equality. We are all different, not necessarily better or worse, but possessed of different talents, different capabilities, different likes and dislikes.

Humility and a positive attitude are the two pillars of wisdom. We have to be humble because we understand so little of what is happening, and we have to have a positive attitude because by and large the conditions of our lives have been gradually improving. We have more security, more understanding, more comfort, and more social concern now than we had in the past.

ॐ

"A prince who is not himself wise cannot be wisely advised … good advice depends on the shrewdness of the prince who seeks it."
—MACHIAVELLI (1469–1527), *The Prince*

"The beginning of wisdom is to call things by their right names."
—CHINESE PROVERB

"The most manifest sign of wisdom is a continual cheerfulness."
—MONTAIGNE (1533–1592)

"Whether you know it or not, my son, the world is governed by very little wisdom."
—COUNT AXEL OXENSTIERNA (1583–1654), Chancellor of Sweden

"Keep the gold and keep the silver, but give us wisdom."
—ARAB PROVERB

INVESTING

In this world, I know of just one phenomenon to which the laws of physics and chemistry do not seem to apply: the stock market.

Gold does not pay interest, but it also does not produce negative returns as many currencies do.

Merchant banking is raising funds to take stakes in companies that a firm is also financing.

It's only possible to achieve a little return at a time by investing. Emerging markets are superheated. During crises they may rapidly become illiquid.

To preserve capital, sometimes stock has to be sold. As we cannot predict the future, we should sell one half of our holdings when a stock doubles. We then have the other half free. Also, consider selling a stock when it represents a fair value.

If you protect the downside, you may get lucky on three or four stocks, and that will take care of the upside.

A fiduciary should manage money as if it were his own.

Errors are inevitable. Expect them and reorganize quickly when they occur. Keep in mind that whenever you invest you are trying to predict the future.

Rites of initiation:
- Find a discipline that works and stick to it. This is the most important decision in investing.
- Do not lose yourself in inconsequentials.
- Question what you believe, or have someone else do it.

Forward-looking valuations: when something looks cheap, it's because it does not seem to represent real value.

Notes from Joseph Wechsberg's (1907–1983) *The Merchant Bankers* (Pocket Books, 1966):
- Francis Baring's secret: find out a little more a little earlier than the next man.

- Progress in thinking is progress toward simplicity. Ex libris Siegmund George Warburg. Warburg has two books in him. One he calls *The Businessman's Book of Quotations*, an outgrowth of his interest in epigrams. Sample: "Influence is more important than power. This applies both to nations and individuals." Warburg's second book, tentatively called *Education for the Adult*, will deal with his favorite thesis that self-education relatively late in life is far more important than school education early in life.
- Happiness is not the fulfillment of desires but the fulfillment of duties.
- Big people gladly pay a premium for lucidity of thought and economy of expression.
- To sell your best assets is poor portfolio management.

Evaluating an investment "opportunity" is judging the difference between the reality and the perception.

᠗

"Perception is reality."

—GEORGE SOROS (1930–)

"Stock selection is much more important than market timing. Investing at market lows and selling at market highs is much less effective than investing in the best group of stocks—irrespective of market averages."

—MICHEL DAVID-WEILL (1932–), Senior Partner, Lazard Frères

"Picking the right fund turns out to be as much hard work as picking the right stock."

—LOUIS RUKEYSER (1933–2006)

From Warren Buffett (1930–), Chairman of Berkshire Hathaway:

- Chairman's Letter, 1988: "Stick within what I call your circle of competence. You have to know what you understand and what you don't understand. Concentrate your investments in a very few companies and try to understand them well. Find a handful of businesses where you have strong long-term convictions. When you find such a business, participate in a meaningful way."

- Annual Meeting, 1994: "Derivatives are a form of extreme leverage: when you combine ignorance and large amounts of borrowed money, you can have some pretty interesting circumstances. ... Concentrate on what will happen, not when. You have to do what works for you."

"Forget dividends. Look for capital gains and trading profits. Do not invest unless the possibilities of the chosen stock seem very great. Safety should come not from selection of a slow mover or a cheap issue or worse yet, a group of such shares, but by concentration in the one outstanding, fast-trading leader that is jumping in the right direction. Do not diversify. Four or five good stocks are enough. Buy only large, liquid companies traded on leading stock exchanges."

—G. M. LOEB (1899–1974), *Battle for Investment Survival,* 1935
(Wiley, 1996)

"He [Siegmund Warburg] often drew an analogy between bankers and physicians. 'Listen to your patients, advise them well and strive to understand not just their special ailments but the whole fellow.' The doctor, he thought, should deliver stern truth, not just flattery. ... Sometimes Siegmund dismissed people by saying, 'Oh my dear fellow, he is not a banker.' By that he meant that the person was a technician, not a rounded financial person with a broad view of events."

—RON CHERNOW (1949–), *The Warburgs* (Random House, 1993)

"Successful investing is like most things in life—to be done well, it must be done thoroughly. ... It's only common sense to study success—not only in investments, but in all facets of life."

—JOHN TEMPLETON (1912–2008)

"If an organization functions well, profitability follows. How did the organization cope with difficulties when they occurred? Shifted product orientation? Do you have confidence in the integrity of the leadership—can you trust them in what they do?"

—HARRY LEVINSON, PHD (1922–2012), career and leadership expert

"There is always something to worry about. Avoid weekend thinking, and ignore the latest dire predictions of newscasters. Sell a stock because the company's fundamentals deteriorate, not because the sky is falling."

—PETER LYNCH (1944–)

"Buy only investments worth substantially more than they cost. Avoid growth stocks, they tend to become overpriced in good markets and to underperform in bad ones. Defensive investors should always have at least 25% of their assets in bonds and at least 25% in equities. When the market is high, debt securities offer better values than equities. Stocks provide better inflation protection than bonds. Do not pay above one-third more than book value. The main benefit of having a professional adviser is to protect the investor from costly mistakes." (FB: Ben Graham [1894–1976] is known as the father of value investing.)

—BENJAMIN GRAHAM, *The Intelligent Investor*
(HarperCollins, 1949; rev. ed., 2003)

"In the mind of the beginner there are many possibilities, in an expert's mind there are few."

—SHUNRIYU SUZUKI (1904–1971)

J

THE JEWISH EXPERIENCE

The most frightening idea of the Holocaust is not that Hitler and his party and friends attempted to kill the Jews and others they considered undesirable, but that they could feel sure of the support, or at least the passivity, of the overwhelming majority of the Germans and the rest of the world.

The American government's canceling of visas of Czechoslovak citizens after Hitler's occupation of Czechoslovakia in March 1939 resulted in the death in concentration camps of most of the people who held them. Thus the U.S. government abetted one of the greatest crimes of the twentieth century, not through active collaboration but through passivity, denial, and indifference.

Once Hitler decided to invade Russia, four-fifths of Germany's armed forces were needed on the eastern front and only one-fifth was left on the western front. Both in terms of casualties inflicted and the amount of materiel consumed, it was the eastern front that saved Western Europe.

Genocide, like all crimes, is ultimately committed (or resisted) by individuals. It is fallacious to confer total collective innocence or guilt on nations because of their past actions.

◦⃗

"Some are guilty; all are responsible."
                              —Rabbi Abraham Herschel (1907–1972)

"Guilt is always personal, not collective, not inherited."

—VICTOR FRANKL (1905–1997)

"Why did the heavens not darken and the stars not withhold their radiance? Why did not the sun and moon turn dark?"

—SALOMON BAR SIMPSON, chronicle 1096, after zealous Christians had killed thousands of Jews on their advance through Germany during the First Crusade

"One is reminded of the medieval chronicler who broke off his work to cry out: 'I am ashamed to tell all that the Cossacks did to us, I am ashamed to tell it for fear of blaspheming the name of man which God created in his image.' For a pious Jew … nothing can be conceived without God. Does it mean that God is present in sadness also? Yes, in sadness also. And perhaps even in absence."

—ELIE WIESEL (1928–2016), *NYT*, January 17, 1988

"There never lived a human being who was not at once a particular and a universal. The obligations of partiality and impartiality are ceaseless and simultaneous … it is sometimes said that the Palestinians are the victims' victims … but if the victims are not to be released from the high human standards then neither are the victims' victims. The wretched, too, must act decently. Otherwise the cruelty will never end."

—LEON WIESELTIER (1952–), *TNR*, September 1997

"In the Jewish tradition, arguing with God is a form of worship."

—NAOMI WOLF (1962–), *TNR*, November 30, 1992

"Being Jewish is a fate, not a faith, and being fate, is inescapable."

—ISIDOR RABI (1898–1988)

"Hatred is not always the enemy of, or the obstacle to, understanding … hatred may be evidence that a state of affairs has been properly understood. ... It is not always true that *tout comprendre c'est tout pardonner.* Comprehension does not always lead to forgiveness. In certain cases, forgiveness may signify the absence of comprehension."

—LEON WIESELTIER (1952–), *TNR*, May 3, 1993

"In Israel, in order to be a realist you must believe in miracles."

—DAVID BEN-GURION (1886–1973)

L

LANGUAGE, LITERATURE, COMMUNICATION

We do not know the exact meaning of many words and phrases we use: personality, character, quality of life, the mind, the spirit. We should try to define them. But can we? What does "sacred" mean when applied to something—that we are not allowed to analyze or describe it?

Much of what happens in human relationships is tied to communications. We need truth and clarity in our communications. Bumper stickers and sweatshirt slogans are no substitute for intellectual discourse.

Most people do not talk to each other; they chat. To talk to each other is to have a real conversation. To avoid being too blunt or getting bored, learn how to ask important questions and how to answer them well.

If an event or statement does not make sense, it is called unreasonable. It is important to differentiate between the unreasonable and the absurd—nonsense statements often sound good.

"Classic" describes something of universal interest that transcends the age we live in. Jargon is the language unimportant people use so they will appear to be important.

There exists nowadays a literary approach whose authors seem to feel that precision in their observations is all-important, while the manner of presentation is unimportant. Not so. An essay should be a text of knowledge and reflection which does not forget that it is also literature.

We no longer feel the absurdity of the lives we have been given to live because we are no longer capable of finding words to express our feelings.

We use storytelling to make sense of our own experience.

About writing:
- Have something to say, say it and stop
- You cannot get to the point if there is no point to get to.

As is always the case with real literature, the ideal of neutrality proves impossible, if only because literary work uses language as its material, and having language is tantamount to making choices between words, figures of speech, types of syntax, and so on.

Poems do not obey Aristotelian logic; they can accommodate several contradictory meanings at the same time.

A good stage play gains credibility as serious drama only if it takes on meaning that cannot be confined to the stage.

When at the opera I often think of Robert Brustein's (1927–) remark: "Any plot too silly to be spoken, along with any event too implausible to be acted, can always be sung." (*TNR*, May 13, 1991)

☙

"The most important function of literature and art is the opening up of imagination."
—THEODORE ZELDIN (1933–), *An Intimate History of Humanity*
(Harper Perennial, 1995)

"The common fluency of speech in many men, and most women, is owing to a scarcity of matter, and a scarcity of words; for whoever is a master of language and has a mind full of ideas, will be apt, in speaking, to hesitate upon the choice of both; whereas common speakers have only one set of ideas and one set of words to clothe them in; and these are always ready at the mouth: so people come faster out of a church when it is almost empty, than when a crowd is at the door."
—JONATHAN SWIFT (1667–1745), *Thoughts on Various Subjects*, 1706

"Poems, like books, are never finished. They are just abandoned in despair and from sheer exhaustion."
—CHARLES BAUDELAIRE (1821–1867)

"When I wrote that, God and I knew what it meant, but now God alone knows."
—ROBERT BROWNING (1812–1899)

"These abbreviators harm both knowledge and love … pandering to impatience, the mother of stupidity."
—LEONARDO DA VINCI (1452–1519)

"It has been a matter of honor to me to make myself obscure to the ignorant, for that is what distinguishes the learned, to speak in a style that seems Greek to the ignorant, for precious pearls should not be cast before swine."
—LUIS DE GONGORA (1561–1627)

"Obscurity does not make a prima facie case for profundity."
—SIR PETER MEDAWAR (1915–1987)

"'The intellectuals could not, of course [writes Carey], actually prevent the masses from attaining literacy. But they could prevent them from

reading literature by making it too difficult for them to understand.'
The obscurity of modernism kept literature (and music and painting)
in the hands of cultured chaps. It kept it out of the hands of clerks,
suburbanites, Eastern European immigrants, and the other nasty
creatures growing in such numbers."

—DEIRDRE N. MCCLOSKEY (1942–), reviewing *The Intellectuals and the
Masses* by John Carey, *Reason*, July 1994

"Sometimes the understanding of the obvious is more important
than the understanding of the obscure, especially when the obvious
counts."

—OLIVER WENDELL HOLMES (1841–1935)

"'Realism' in the highest sense of the word does not intend to copy the
reality of the world: its significance is based on its endeavor to express
the whole world of a human being in the expression of his thoughts, in
the fight between good and evil. The place where this war takes place is
the human heart."

—DOSTOEVSKY (1821–1881)

"The true enemy of man is generalization."

—CZESLAW MILOSZ (1911–2004)

"If the meaning of words is not clear, language is without an object.
When language is without an object, no affairs can be effected.
Therefore whatever a gentleman conceives of, he must be able to say;
and whatever he says, he must be able to do. In the matter of language,
a gentleman leaves nothing to chance."

—CONFUCIUS (551–479 BCE), *Analects*, tr. Simon Leys (Norton, 1997)

"The way you define a problem will determine what you do about it."

—JONATHAN MANN (1947–1998)

"His great skill lay in defining problems in ways that seemed amenable to solution. Clarity of thought and expression was almost a moral duty."
                    —CHARLES HOPE on E. H. Gombrich, *NYR*, December 20, 2001

"Exaggeration is the spice of conversation."
                                        —LOUIS CHEDID, MD

"Nothing can be more a waste of time than a serious subject trifled with, nothing better worthwhile than nonsense turned to good account."
                    —DESIDERIUS ERASMUS (1466–1536), in a letter to
                                Sir Thomas More, June 12, 1508

"Literature is useless against reality while being a great consolation to the individual."
                                —ROMAIN ROLLAND (1866–1944)

"Never trust the artist. Trust the tale. The proper function of a critic is to save the tale from the artist who created it."
                                —D. H. LAWRENCE (1885–1930)

"Change the name, and the tale is about you."
                                —HORACE (65–8 BCE)

"To allow others to share in the astonishment of being, the dazzlement of existence, and to shout to God and other human beings our anguish, letting it be known that we were there."
            —EUGENE IONESCO (1909–1994), on why he wanted to be a writer

"Literature does not proceed like science. It draws upon other means to lead to knowledge. The writer can project himself into the souls of people, historical or fictitious, and bring us revelations which, even if they remain unproven, can sometimes enlighten more than the long

accumulation of facts produced by the historian, the psychologist or the sociologist. Through the shortcuts of intuition and imagination, the writer can succeed where the scientist fails."
—TZVETAN TODOROV (1939–2017), *TNR*, November 18, 1996

"If you would not be forgotten,
As soon as you are dead and rotten,
Either write things worthy of reading,
Or do things worth the writing."
—BENJAMIN FRANKLIN (1706–1790), *Poor Richard's Almanack*, 1738

LAWS, RULES, APHORISMS

Laws

Gresham's Law: The inferior currency will drive out the superior because of the hoarding of the latter. (As adapted by FB: Irrelevant issues drive out relevant ones.)
—SIR THOMAS GRESHAM (1519–1579)

Hume's Law: No statements about value can logically be derived purely from statements about facts. No statement about what ought to be can be derived exclusively from statements about what is, was, or will be the case. (FB: You cannot derive an ought from an is.)

Hume's Razor: No testimony is sufficient to establish a miracle unless that testimony be of such a kind that its falsehood would be more miraculous than the fact which it endeavors to establish.
—DAVID HUME (1711–1776)

Occam's Razor: If a simple solution is available, it is always preferable to more complicated explanations.

—WILLIAM OF OCCAM, Doctor Singularis et Invincibilis (1288–1347)

Parkinson's Law: Work expands so as to fill the time available for its completion.

—C. NORTHCOTE PARKINSON (1909–1993)

The Peter Principle: In a hierarchy, every employee tends to rise to his level of incompetence. The cream rises until it sours.

—LAWRENCE J. PETER (1920–1990)

Say's Law: Supply creates its own demand.

—JEAN-BAPTISTE SAY (1767–1832)

Useful Rules

1) *Do a sensitivity analysis.* Concentrate efforts only on those aspects of a problem that have the potential to affect the outcome.
2) *Adopt long-term orientation.* Business-school graduates are trained advocates of short-term profits.
3) *Set realistic goals.* Do not demand more than is possible from yourself or others. Avoid the perils of perfectionism.
4) *Take problems and situations at face value.* Do not assume the existence of hidden forces or motives.

And:
- Never apologize, never explain.
- Never attribute to malice what can be adequately explained by stupidity.
- Always be a little kinder than is necessary.
- Stop doing what does not work.

- "Beware," goes the proverb, "lest you receive your heart's desire."

There is only one supreme rule: surviving without harming others.

&

"Don't let the best be the enemy of the good. Good is good enough. Do not get distracted seeking perfection."
—VOLTAIRE (1694–1778), 1764

"Be tough with institutions and gentle with people."
—MAX HAMILTON (1912–1988)

"Cooperate with the inevitable."
—ASHLEY MONTAGU (1905–1999)

"Always endeavor to really be what you would wish to appear."
—FRANCIS BACON (1561–1626)

"Never mind what color the cat is, as long as it gets the mouse."
—CHINESE PROVERB

"Never compound a misfortune or error." (FB: If a pro tennis player thinks he's had a bad decision, he may become so upset he loses the match by making further errors.)
—HENRY HAZLITT (1894–1993)

"You can't get tired dancing with a bear; you have to wait until the bear gets tired."
—RUSSIAN PROVERB

Aphorisms from Known and Unknown Sources

"Only the mediocre are always at their best."

—JEAN GIRAUDOUX (1882–1944)

"Nothing can prevent some seats in the theatre being better than others."

—CHRYSIPPUS (280–207 BCE)

"A drain inspector's work is bound to smell of drains."

—GANDHI (1869–1948)

"Virtue consists of a mean between excess and deficiency."

—ARISTOTLE (384–322 BCE)

"In matters of grave importance, style, not sincerity, is the vital thing."

—OSCAR WILDE (1854–1900)

"All things excellent are as difficult as they are rare."

—SPINOZA (1632–1677)

"The fools are dancing, but the even bigger fools are watching."

—JAPANESE PROVERB

Everything goes on longer than you think it will.

In any complex system, speed of progress is limited by the slowest moving part.

The exception destroys the rule.

LIFE: MEANING, PURPOSE, QUALITY

Meaning

People like to do things that will accomplish more than merely advancing their position in life. They follow such pursuits in a search for meaning. But since we cannot determine with any degree of certainty whether a higher spiritual being, a "God," exists, we cannot determine whether there is a god-given purpose or meaning to our lives. This does not mean that our minds have no spiritual aspects; we want our lives to have purpose and meaning because to live without them is boring. So we try to provide purpose and meaning by caring for our families and clinging to our religion and our country. To find the meaning of life, people may also travel great distances or use drugs or other ways of changing their state of consciousness.

As I see it, life has no meaning, but our obligation and privilege is, to quote Elie Wiesel (1928–2016), "to give meaning to life and in doing so to overcome the passive, indifferent life." Though death has no meaning, life can have it. The point of view of the Ethical Culture movement is: We do not find meaning in the universe. We give meaning to life; it is our task to make life meaningful.

Life isn't something that merely happened to you; it is something you made happen. How can we make our own insignificant lives worthwhile? By helping to create some value that was not there before.

One of the prerequisites of a happy life is to find out what is meaningful and important to oneself and then arrange things so that one can act on these discoveries. We have to be what we want to be. Life should be seen as a challenge to fully develop our human potential. Said Goethe (1749–1832): "When you take your needs seriously, you are on the right track."

The problem is that for many people the most important thing in life is to attract attention by trying to prove or imply that they are the best informed, the wisest, the bravest, or the most miserable.

❧

Humans have a basic need to relate to goals that are beyond those involved in the goal of simple survival."

—MARK DAVIDSON, *Uncommon Sense: The Life and Thought of Ludwig von Bertalanffy* (Tarcher, 1983)

"People say that what we're all seeking is a meaning for life ... I think that what we're seeking is an experience of being alive, so that our life experiences on the purely physical plane will have resonances with our own innermost being and reality. ... What's the meaning of the universe? What's the meaning of a flea? It's just there. That's it. And your own meaning is that you're there. We're so engaged in doing things to achieve purposes of *outer* value that we forget ... the inner value, the rapture that is associated with being alive ..."

—JOSEPH CAMPBELL (1904–1987), *The Power of Myth* with Bill Moyers (1934–) (Doubleday, 1988)

"I see life as a dance. Does dance have to have a meaning? You are dancing because you enjoy it."

—JACKIE MASON (1931–)

"In this life I am God, and like God, I am indifferent to my own fate."

  —HENRY MILLER (1891–1980), *On Writing* (New Directions, 1964)

Purpose

It is well to make up one's mind about how one is going to operate in life—by principles or by self-interest. (It is of course possible to operate in a third way—by inconsequentials: Where do I sit in a restaurant? Am I a member of the "in" group?)

We are placed here to be companions—a wonderful word that comes from the Latin *cum panis* (with bread). We are here to share bread with one another.

Not everything has a purpose. What is the purpose of the sky, of magnetism, of dandelions, or of Mont Blanc? Why then should we ask what the purpose of life is? Or why should the universe have a purpose?

                  ☙

"The majority prove their worth by keeping busy. A busy life is the nearest thing to a purposeful life."

  —ERIC HOFFER (1902–1983), *In Our Time* (Harper & Row, 1976)

"You are here to enrich the world, and you impoverish yourself if you forget the errand."

      —WOODROW WILSON (1856–1924)

"Three Mantras: Do what you can. Want what you have. Be who you are."
—FORREST CHURCH (1948–2009)

"Look ahead. You are not expected to complete the task. Neither are you permitted to lay it down."
—THE TALMUD

"I tell you we are here on earth to fart around, and don't let anybody tell you any different."
—KURT VONNEGUT (1922–2007)

"The true joy of life lies in being used for a mighty purpose and being a force of nature instead of a feverish, selfish little clod of ailments and grievances complaining that the world will not devote itself to making you happy."
—GEORGE BERNARD SHAW (1856–1950),
Man and Superman, 1903

"I cannot believe that the purpose of life is to be happy. I think the purpose of life is to be useful, to be responsible, to be compassionate. It is, above all, to matter, to count, to stand for something, to have made some difference that you lived at all."
—LEO ROSTEN (1908–1997)

"What a man actually needs is not a tensionless state but rather the striving and struggling for some goal worthy of him."
—VICTOR FRANKL (1905–1997)

"I began to believe that the purpose of my life was not to be a 'people-pleaser.' I began to learn how to count on myself, how to please myself, how to be myself. I stopped being for everybody except me."
—KATIE CANNON (1949–), in *God's Fierce Whimsy*
(Pilgrim Press, 1985)

"If you have tried to build castles in that air your work need not be lost; that is where they should be. Now put the foundations under them."
—HENRY DAVID THOREAU (1817–1862),
"Life Without Principle," 1854

"No man can set in order the details unless he has already set before himself the chief purpose of his life. … Our plans miscarry because they have no aim. When a man does not know what harbor he is making for, no wind is the right wind."
—SENECA (4 BCE–65 CE)

"If you don't know where you are going, any road will take you there."
—LEWIS CARROLL (1832–1898)

"The adventure that the hero is ready for is the one he gets."
—JOSEPH CAMPBELL (1904–1987)

Quality

Quality of life is the measure of the satisfactions that make one's life worthwhile.

In his *History of the Idea of Progress,* Robert Nisbet (1913–1996) identified five "crucial premises" that make living worthwhile and sustain the idea of progress—of which he said, "no single idea has been more important … in Western civilization for three thousand years." They are "1) belief in the value of the past; 2) conviction of the nobility, even superiority, of Western civilization; 3) acceptance of the worth of economic and technological growth; 4) faith in reason and the kind of scientific and scholarly knowledge that can come from reason alone; 5) belief in the intrinsic importance, the ineffaceable worth, of life on earth." (Basic Books, 1980)

We cannot control the events that profoundly influence our lives, but we must not permit this to make us feel helpless. Emotional immaturity is the inability or unwillingness to understand that life is not necessarily as we think it should be, and a refusal to accept the fact that we cannot change the world around us to any large extent. An emotionally mature person recognizes that there are still many ways in which a satisfying life can be lived in this imperfect world.

Before accepting advice from anybody about happiness, success, or enjoyment of life, ask yourself a simple question: How did the adviser succeed in his own life? How did the advice he is giving you help him?

The wisdom of living in the present has been known for centuries. As Epicurus (341–270 BCE) said, "The fool with all his other thoughts has this also: He is always getting ready to live."

In Athens in the late fifth century BC, the three essential things for a good life were: 1) good health; 2) good looks; and 3) being rich without cheating.

Savoir vivre—To know how to live well: grace, style, manners

&

Ubi bene, ibi patria—Where I am at ease, there is my country.

—LATIN SAYING

"There are three ingredients in the good life: learning, earning and yearning."

—CHRISTOPHER MORLEY (1890–1957)

"I derive my worldview from a dry cleaner's slip: 'Some stains can only be removed by the destruction of the material itself.'"

—BOHUMIL HRABAL (1914–1997)

"The tragedy of life is not so much what men suffer, but rather what they miss."

—THOMAS CARLYLE (1795–1881)

"The four things I rather have: to be out of jail, to eat regular, to get what I write printed, and then a little love at home and a little outside."

—CARL SANDBURG (1878–1967)

"I have tried haltingly, inadequately but sincerely … to repay through service some of the debt I owe to life for its profuse bounty towards me."

—RABBI DAVID DE SOLA POOL (1885–1970), in *This I Believe: Documents of American Jewish Life* (Jason Aronson, 1990)

"Whatever we do, we ask ourselves silently whenever there is a pause: Is this really the most I can get out of life, is this really the most I can get out of the few years left in this one life of mine?"

—JOSEPH HELLER (1923–1999), *Something Happened* (Simon & Schuster, 1974)

"We are all guilty of the crime of not living life to the full."

—HENRY MILLER (1891–1980), *Sexus* (Grove Press, 1949)

"Whatever it is that pulls the pin, that hurls you past the boundaries of your own life into a brief and total beauty, even for a moment, it is enough."

—JEANETTE WINTERSON (1959–), *Gut Symmetries* (Knopf, 1997)

LOVE, FIDELITY, MARRIAGE, SEXUALITY

Love

The hallmarks of psychological maturity are the abilities to love and to work.

There are three different kinds of love: Eros, the erotic love; philia, which comprises compassion and affection; and agape, which is love devoted to the good of the loved one. There is an element of each in every love relationship.

Love:
- is like Ping Pong. The game is all over once you stop returning the ball.
- is unconditional and nonjudgmental and exists for its own sake. It has no purpose.
- should not be declared, it should be acted out: deeds, not fine words.
- is more rewarding than sex in the long run, just as wisdom is more precious than riches. Yet we have to live in the short run too.
- is two things: acceptance and support. The acceptance is unconditional and the support absolute. The support implies assistance under all circumstances, and absolute loyalty.
- is an experience of delight, harmony, and a feeling of intense union.

Love comes at a time when the lover needs to share his solitude with someone who can make it bearable. Complete love between a man and a woman includes sex, but sex is not its chief ingredient.

Romantic love fades; intimate affection lasts.

Human relationships are based mainly on self-interest. This also applies to love, but it is absurd to reduce love to selfishness. The joy of love is being able to give and to receive at the same time.

The capacity to relinquish control is a key to the ability to love. Accept those you love just the way they are. The best thing we can do for those we love is to set them free to be themselves.

Deal with your relationships without pretending to be someone you aren't. Overcome fear of rejection and need for approval.

You never love anybody until you love somebody more than yourself. Self-sufficiency is not the same as not needing anyone.

Never compare countries or women. Enjoy each one fully for what they are.

&

"Love consists of this: that two solitudes protect and touch and greet one another. … Once the realization is accepted that even between the closest human beings infinite distances continue to exist, a wonderful living side by side can grow up if they succeed in loving the distance between them which makes it possible for each to see the other whole against the sky."
—RAINER MARIA RILKE (1875–1926)

"My message to those I love and cherish: if I can do it, so can you. If you would be loved, love and be lovable."
—BENJAMIN FRANKLIN (1706–1790)

"The great tragedy of life is not that men perish, but that they cease to love."
—W. SOMERSET MAUGHAM (1874–1965)

"His characters suffer and lose sleep and (almost, but not quite) die from love. Yet they know that love is all we have against death, against old age, which [says one], wastes us, hour by hour."
—FRANCINE PROSE on Chaucer, *NYT*, February 14, 1988

"A man who charms a woman thinks he has acquired her, whereas a relationship of love should involve a new charm every day. Men do not like the idea that love is only the basis for doing other things. Love is not the solution to all problems, it is only a starting point: then many more choices have to be made."
—THEODORE ZELDIN (1933–), *An Intimate History of Humanity* (Harper Perennial, 1995)

Fidelity

The proof of love is loyalty, not fidelity. Relationships should be based on commitment, not feelings. Feelings change from day to day but commitment is an act of trust, a promise that should not be broken without good reason.

Affairs—which can be real or imaginary—can hold marriages together.

Much of modern literature is an embellishment of the well-known observation that interest in sex can decrease over time when engaged in with the same person. This often happens in marriage. Among the ways of dealing with the problem are: lose interest in sex, get a divorce, find a lover.

One great contribution of French culture is its attitude toward infidelity. They made it acceptable and in doing so stabilized the family. American society, in regarding it as a cardinal sin, generated a divorce rate of more than 50 percent.

Why should sex be called sinful? Both men and women have the right to, and should be able to, enjoy carefree sex with any other consenting adult without binding consequences. It has nothing to do with love or marriage. But each action has consequences, and those involved in the act must be aware of them and take responsibility.

Fidelity is not a virtue; it is a preference.

One of the secrets of a good sexual relationship is freedom from excessive control.

Jealousy has nothing to do with love. It has to do with sexual betrayal.

Male orangutans are faithful and devoted to their mates and families. The chimpanzees (more closely related to man) like to have new females after a few sexual experiences.

తి

"Don Juan: How can you ask me to be faithful to you? That would mean being cruel to my girlfriend!"

—LORENZO DA PONTE (1749–1838), librettist,
Mozart's *Don Giovanni*

"Do you believe in monogamy? When monogamy was invented, life expectancy was very much shorter than now. Seriously, it is the best option if your marriage, like mine, is full of love and is perpetually refreshed and reinvented. Otherwise, it is better to part before you die alive."

—ABDALLAH S. DAAR, *The Lancet,* November 4, 2000

"Few would dare to comment on genital selection, or to discuss with their students the reasons for suspecting that human beings are basically a polygynous primate, like the gorilla (under the cloak of serial monogamy)."

— *The Lancet*, Editorial, December 23–30, 1995

"The art of being wise is the art of knowing what to overlook."

—WILLIAM JAMES (1842–1910)

Marriage and Divorce

The purpose of marriage is threefold: having children, civilizing young males, and having somebody to fall back on. The second and third aims can also be expressed by making each other secure and happy.

Marriage should provide completeness that the partners lack separately. The essence of this completeness is more psychic than physical.

In the past it was death that undermined the family; now it is divorce. The dramatic rise in the divorce rate during the last 100 years is merely a compensatory mechanism for the contemporaneous decline in the adult mortality rate.

☙

"Marriage is the union of two persons of different sexes for the purpose of lifelong mutual possession of their sexual organs."

—IMMANUEL KANT (1724–1804)

"It was not so much what he gave you as what he did not take away."
—GERTRUDE STEIN (1874–1946)

"Remarriage: The triumph of hope over experience."
—SAMUEL JOHNSON (1709–1784)

"A man who is married and loses his wife and marries again does not deserve the sad look he had the first time."
—OSCAR WILDE (1854–1900)

Sexuality

The big problems in life that confront everyone are the three S's: security, safety, and sex. It is desirable to have a secure job and all that brings; to be safe and unconcerned about violence, persecution, or humiliation; and to have sex, which, as many suspect, can give more pleasure and satisfaction than anything else.

Sex is separate from love, although it can make love grow or be part of love.

Religion and government try to make sex degradingly necessary.

Free speech, free trade, and free sex all go together.

We teach everything—French, math, art, philosophy. There is just one subject that is not properly taught and that is sex. We are rarely if ever stimulated to find out what math, art, philosophy, and all the rest of the subjects being taught are all about. The only subject for which our appetite is being continuously whetted is sex. Yet this is the field about which little else except misleading information is available.

Sex has no moral dimension. Sex should be done for sex's sake. No other justification is needed.

To paraphrase Samuel Johnson: anyone who is tired of sex is tired of life.

Work should not be a substitute for sex.

Sex is mental. If sex is not satisfactory, there is a problem of communication between minds.

Sexual dysfunction is the presenting problem; the real problem is what is happening in one's life.

Sexuality has more to do with taking pleasure from stimulation of genital organs and the body than with reproduction and cannot be defined solely in terms of reproduction.

Sex is not the way we prove our commitment. People can deeply care for one another and have a relationship based on respect and love, not necessarily on sex. Sex satisfies an urge.

One of the nicest aspects of intimate relationships is the freedom to be yourself. When you are afraid to let yourself go, you close the door to one of the most satisfying and rewarding aspects of living. "Game playing" and pretense inhibit genuine feelings of closeness.

Masturbation feels good. The problem is that you always know what the next move is going to be. The essence of enjoyment in sex is novelty.

Nocturnal emissions and sex dreams are symptoms of sex deprivation. Fasting decimates the body, sexual abstention decimates the spirit. After a few days of fasting, the appetite is lost and eating is no longer enjoyed. The same follows for sexual abstinence.

When people learn that one may acquire AIDS by having sex, they are relieved of their regrets for not having had enough sex in the past.

In Aristophanes' (446–386 BCE) *Assembly of Women*, the older Athenian women, because of their very repulsiveness, have a right to enjoy handsome young men before beautiful young women do.

We are interested in sex not only because of the sex drive but also because of our indomitable appetite for experience.

Thomas Aquinas equated human sexuality with brutish animal reproductive mating, but why should people be ashamed of their sexual feelings? Did not the creator implant these into us? The sex drive is an inborn instinct—we have no choice in the matter—so why be ashamed of it? This is a birthright. It is desired by everyone. True sexuality has the capability of ameliorating the natural aloneness of the human condition. It has the ability to replenish the human soul.

☙

"The mind has no sex."

—Francois Poulain de la Barre (1647–1723)

"Free expression of every passion—homosexuality, polygamy, unfettered sexual drives—would create social harmony and bring about a new social order."

—Charles Fourier (1772–1837)

"The ability to make love frivolously is the chief characteristic which distinguishes human beings from the beasts."

—HEYWOOD BROUN (1888–1939)

"An intellectual is someone who has discovered something more interesting than sex."

—ALDOUS HUXLEY (1894–1963)

"The thing (sex) is a sensory pleasure, that is, an event occurring within one's own body ... we say of a lustful man prowling the streets that he wants a woman. [But] he wants a pleasure for which a woman happens to be the necessary piece of apparatus. How much he cares about the woman as such may be gauged by his attitude to her five minutes after fruition. ... Now Eros makes a man really want, not a woman, but one particular woman."

—C. S. LEWIS (1898–1963), *The Four Loves*
(Harvest Books, 1960)

"I have never seen a man who loved virtue as much as sex."

—CONFUCIUS (551–479 BCE), *Analects*,
tr. Simon Leys (Norton, 1997)

M

MEDIA, ADVERTISING, MIND MANIPULATION

Media

Fear is the cheapest commodity to fabricate and the easiest to sell at great profit. The manufacturers, wholesalers, and retailers of fear have been the major impediment to the enlightenment of the human race throughout history.

H. L. Mencken (1880–1956) said, "The curse of man, and the cause of nearly all his woes, is his stupendous capacity for believing the incredible." And from Oliver Wendell Holmes (1841–1935): "The most far-reaching form of power is not money, it is the command of ideas."

The media profoundly affect the public perception of what is good or bad, desirable or undesirable, and of what life is all about.

What can make life frightening is the often wholesale success of the media in promoting accusations unsupported by any visible or tangible evidence. This is dangerous since we have the ability to think selectively—i.e., to focus on lines of reasoning that support a particular conclusion and ignore those that do not. We are thus capable of believing anything we want to, are willing to, or can be induced to believe. This fact gives the media the power to incline us to believe anything *they* want us to believe. Manipulating this power is evil. We should learn to resist overwhelming propaganda.

The meaning of facts depends on how we interpret them. What the public makes of political events depends upon the framework within which they are viewed.

American media treat complexity the way Victorians treated sexuality— as something from which the viewer and the reader need to be protected. Historian Jacob Burkhardt (1818-1897) said of his own era, "Ours would be the age of 'the great simplifiers' and the essence of tyranny is the denial of complexity."

The sensationalism of the mass media is a real danger to progress.

In every era and in every country, public opinion is conformist and complacent; it does not take kindly to those who unsettle it.

Our media have a hidden bias against labor, women, and minorities and often treat them as special interest groups. Pro-business viewpoints proliferate on both commercial and public TV.

Don't believe anything until it has been officially denied three times.

Advertising

Thoughts on advertising:
- Consumer demand is frequently based on misinformation.
- This misinformation is made acceptable by inducing fear.
- It creates the belief that fate and misfortune can be avoided if gods are propitiated by eating bran or taking vitamins or by not drinking coffee or alcohol, etc.
- Consumer demand is generated and pushed along by mercantile interests and the insecurity and cynicism of middlemen.

The basic ad markets are beer, pharmaceuticals, cars, and insurance. Most of the so-called educated people are greatly affected by them as in the "Beverly Hills syndrome:" you are what you drive.

If you read the newspapers or watch television, you get the feeling that we could be rich, successful, and happy if we would just access them regularly. The media also make the case that disease and hunger could be wiped out if we would increase our charitable contributions to those causes, and that marriages could be happy and crime disappear if we would stop using drugs, including alcohol, and start going to church regularly.

Advertising is trying to get us to perform certain actions by associating them with such basic interests as sex. Advertisers try to exploit our sexual responsiveness by associating it with commercial products. This is objectionable because it trivializes our deepest feelings and urges. We are being treated like Pavlov's dogs. The advertisers are trying to diminish our powers of reflection upon and choice over what goes into our consciousness.

❧

"The prime objective of television is to hold the viewer's attention, by whatever means proves most expedient, long enough to sell products."
> —Shervert Frazier, MD, *Psychotrends* (Simon & Schuster, 1994)

"Advertising [of medicines should] give information about diseases and alternative treatments rather than pushing a single product. Patients deserve reliable information on available treatments."
> —*The Economist,* August 8, 1998

Mind Manipulation and its Consequences

The ultimate "persuasions" occur in prison camps. In *Prisoner of Mao* by Jean Pasqualini and Rudolph Chelminski (Penguin, 1975), about Pasqualini's years in Chinese labor camps, he describes the psychological techniques used to coerce the innocent and the guilty into submission: months of interrogation and forced confessions. Prisoners were manipulated to use daily criticism of others and confessions of their own wrongdoing until each genuinely believed whatever the authority told them, including their own guilt. Said Pasqualini: "The aim of the authorities is not so much to make you invent nonexistent crimes, but to make you accept your ordinary life, as you live it, as rotten and sinful and worthy of punishment." (FB: This can be seen in our media and advertising, in churches, and especially in cults. We lose the ability to reason independently and go from defiance and skepticism to acceptance, to an enthusiastic embrace of the message.)

"Without civilized institutions, human nature is naked and raw," wrote Victor Brombert (1924–) in a review of a biography of Italian writer and Auschwitz survivor Primo Levi. Levi had described "the monstrous Nazi machine for reducing human beings to beasts before dispatching them to the gas chambers" and "the contaminating conditions under which victims are tempted into becoming accomplices in the atrocities committed against them." (*NYT*, January 24, 1999)

❧

"Intellectual garbage is more dangerous (than material garbage) for it poisons the mind. And people with poisoned minds are capable of acts whose consequences may be irreversible."

—Ivan Klíma (1931–), *The Spirit of Prague*
(Granta Books, 1994)

"To do evil a human being must first of all believe that what he is doing is good. ... Ideology—that is what gives devildoing its long-sought justification and gives the evildoer the necessary steadfast-ness and determination."

—ALEXANDER SOLZHENITSYN (1918–2008)

"We all grew blinders. We trained ourselves to see things in a perspective that did not correspond to reality. We did our thinking strictly within a closed, logical system that had as little to do with the real world as the equally strict and twisted logic of schizophrenics ... we denied that we had been defeated, and we proved logically that we had not been. ... We dared not rock the boat. ... The suppression of all criticism, the insistence of unconditional assent, the dictatorship of the word has wrought immeasurably greater havoc than any kind of free and responsible criticism has ever done."

—ARTHUR KOESTLER (1905–1983), in his "Second Letter of Resignation" from the German Communist Party in 1938, quoted by Michael Scammell, *TNR*, May 4, 1998

MEDICINE

We need to understand that not all illnesses can be accurately diagnosed, that not all conditions can be treated, and that not all treatments are effective.

The third medical revolution is upon us. This revolution ties together mind and health, which the World Health Organization defines as a dynamic state of complete physical, mental, spiritual, and social well-being, not merely the absence of disease or infirmity. Your behavior, your beliefs, and your relationship with the world and the people around you are essential components of your life and your health. When we do not deal with our emotional needs (especially our stresses), we may be setting ourselves up for an illness.

Aging is inevitable, but disease is preventable and modifiable. It is impossible to define it as having an existence independent of our ability to interpret it. Most scientists operate on the assumption that there is a basic order to the nature of things and that it is the purpose of their research to reveal it.

Thoughts on medicine

- Good medicine should be evidence-based. Alternative medicine normally is not. Complementary medicine is a better name than alternative medicine.
- The great books of the past and the present hold the truth of our civilization, the truth that should be known by those who would presume to heal their fellows.
- The first rule of therapeutics: If you can't prove it works, don't do it.
- Treat diseases, not symptoms. Routine treatment of symptoms may be detrimental.
- In medicine Hippocrates' dictum, *Primum nil nocere*, still applies: First, do no harm.
- Medicine not only interprets our symptoms but also in many cases shapes them.
- Galen's view rests on the understanding of disease mechanisms and scientific insight.
- Build on the strength people already have. To remedy weakness is often impossible.
- Subvert unsubstantiated beliefs.
- This is not the best of all possible worlds: the only cells with the property of immortality are not normal cells but tumor cells.

- The joy of medicine, like that of love and friendship, is being able to give and receive at the same time.

&

"Medicine is not science, and it is certainly not art, meaning that the daily practice of medicine is not a scientific activity but a practical craft to ease the many transitions in our lives, from birth to senescence, and to postpone or alleviate some of the worst. However, the progress of medicine is a scientific activity, rooted in both basic and clinical sciences."

— *The Lancet*, Editorial, October 30, 1993

"Infectious diseases are truly global in that no country or population is unaffected. … Thinking big about some scientific (including medical) research means thinking globally and that would prove that there really is intelligent life on earth, wherever else it may or may not be found."

— *The Lancet*, Editorial, August 17, 1986

Diagnosis/Treatment

When confronted with a clinical problem—and every disease or illness can be a clinical problem—we must, as described by Harold C. Sox (*NEJM*, January 29, 1987), make "a decision with consequences that cannot be foretold with certainty … based on probability, the most useful way to quantify uncertainty." The probability, he wrote, should apply to "a specific patient, not the average patient." That is, it is as important to know the person *with* the disease as it is to know the disease. Medical decision analysis should also consider all possible outcomes.

In *Principles of Biomedical Ethics* (Oxford University Press, 1994), T. L. Beauchamps and J. F. Childress describe the four basic principles of bioethics: beneficence, nonmaleficence [do no harm], autonomy, and justice. These principles are not compatible. An example: a terminal cancer patient wants invasive interventions stopped to preserve his autonomy. If his physician complies, he will shorten the patient's life, i.e., produce harm. Or should he refuse and obey nonmaleficence? The context, circumstances, intentions, and consequences have to be taken into consideration because the four basic bioethical principles cannot be applied together.

A doctor should always remember that what is important is not what sort of disease a person has, but that the disease manifests itself differently in each patient, and what works well as a treatment for one person may not work for others.

In short, we have to look for things we cannot measure in a test tube. The manifestations of disease are often the result of strange combinations and interactions of people, moods, beliefs, objects, and places that affect our physiology and biochemistry. The severity and course of a disease can be affected by the life events of the patient. To uncover these peculiar influences, ask patients these questions: What are you doing in your life that you should not be doing? What should you be doing in your life that you are not? What is your greatest concern? What do you think is the worst possibility?

One of the dogmas in medicine today is that treatment must not be instituted until a diagnosis is made. With respect to acute pain, it is a myth that administration of an analgesic may obscure the diagnosis. The goal in medicine is to relieve suffering and to maintain good health, not to diagnose.

The three medical aphorisms of British heart researcher Sir John McMichael (1904–1993): 1) If a drug is doing a patient good, leave well alone; 2) If a drug is not doing good, change it; 3) Never send your patients to surgeons.

☙

"And it will fall out as in a complication of diseases, that by applying a remedy to one sore, you will provoke another; and that which removes the one ill symptom produces others."

—Sir Thomas More (1478–1535)

"To array a man's will against his sickness is the supreme art of medicine."

—Henry Ward Beecher (1813–1887)

"A certain disregard, even contempt, for our minor ailments is a therapy not used often enough. We know what human beings can put up with in situations of severe stress (jail, war, etc.). Read the case reports of those who survived the Holocaust."

—Hervé Maisonneuve, *The Lancet*, January 9, 1999

"Although predicting is perilous, not predicting is even more perilous. It leaves us unprepared for the changes going on right under our noses, confronts us with recurrent surprises, and most problematic, makes us reactors to change instead of agents of change."

—Jerome P. Kassirer, MD (1932–),
NEJM, January 5, 1995

"Our ability to unveil the mysteries of health and diseases and to develop ingenious interventions has far outstripped our ability to use that information."

—D. M. Eddy, MD, *Bulletin of the American College of Surgeons,*
77:36, 1992

"Don't deny the diagnosis, just defy the verdict that is supposed to go with it."

—Norman Cousins (1915–1990),
Advances in Mind-Body Medicine, 1989

"There is no curing those who choose to be diseased."

—Samuel Smiles (1812–1904)

Doctor: Disease v. Patient: Illness

There are no such beings as patients, only people. Most people who come to see a doctor are normal people who have been made anxious by life situations. Every patient who comes to us saying he is experiencing a crisis is indeed experiencing a crisis; he would not be looking for help if he did not sense danger to his well-being. The danger may not be real, but it is real to the patient. Even though getting upset does not solve the problem, it is okay to get upset.

So in a medical consultation there are not one but two experts present: the patient and the doctor. Sherwin Nuland, MD, wrote that "Arthur Kleinman [author of *The Illness Narratives,* 1988] has defined disease as the problem as seen from the point of view of the doctor, and illness as the problem as seen from the point of view of the person who is sick. ... Essentially, then, a disease consists of the microscopically or chemically demonstrable manifestations of a pathological process ...

objective [and] verifiable by others. An illness, by contrast, is the total of the psychological, social and cultural ways in which the sick person experiences the bodily changes caused by the disease." (*TNR*, October 13, 1997)

Physicians today tend to treat the disease and disregard the illness. They have become masters of detached observation of the patient's symptoms, fluids, and images but less than masters at observing the patient.

Along with the dilemma of functional disorders—"I am suffering/ you are not ill"—there is a difference between pain and suffering. Edwin S. Shneidman, PhD, said, "In human beings pain is ubiquitous, but suffering is optional, within the constraints of a person's personality." (*NEJM*, March 26, 1992) Physician and patient may also not share the same values, e.g., valuing survival above quality of life or vice versa.

☙

"Always listen to the patient, not only listen to his story but confide to him one's own, since only through stories can one person fully enter another's life. 'You tell me your story and I'll tell you mine.'"
                    —WILLIAM CARLOS WILLIAMS, MD and poet (1883–1963)

"Lister's rule of good medical practice: put yourself in the patient's place. Patients want efficiency, kindness, understanding and gentleness; and if they have to go through a major ordeal they want to feel that this is only what the doctors involved would want for themselves or their own families. This is what counts."
                    —THURSTON B. BREWIN (1921–2001), *The Lancet*, January 16, 1993

Conditions

There are no local diseases. All diseases are systemic. Cancer of the breast is not a disease of the breast; the whole body is sick.

Treatment of cancer exchanges the disease of cancer for the disease of treatment.

Illness is often a metaphor. Cancer is often saddled with connotations of embarrassment or punishment. This is even more true of AIDS.

Many headaches are a reaction to the individual's hostility toward something, or a feeling of frustration about something. Do headache remedies elevate frustration threefold?

છૈ

"A normal phase of life should not be medicalized by defining menopause as a disease.
— *The Lancet,* Commentary, August 9, 2003

When and What to Tell

We must not deflate anyone's hope. Outcomes cannot be predicted with any certainty. Odds-making is for bookies. Physicians should instill hope. Hope is often all a patient has. Who am I to take it away?

With patients suffering from an incurable disease, decisions about how much to tell the patient, and when, rest not on abstract ethical principles, which vary according to the philosophical stance from which they are proposed, but on a very concrete assessment of the patient, including his medical background, his hopes, his beliefs, his personality, and his fortitude. No previous assumption of what is good and what is evil is acceptable—only what benefits the individual patient. No general ethical stance will ever cover what he needs.

ॐ

"Secrecy entails intentional concealment. Bok [Sissela Bok, author of *Secrets* (Pantheon, 1983)] places secrecy in ordinary social conduct between lying and truthfulness. Harboring secrets about patients stands to rob them of their autonomy, shatter their faith in the physician and open the door to deceit and wrongdoing by those who pass on the secrets."

—JOHN F. BURNUM, *NEJM*, April 18, 1991

"Doctors, like most other professionals, need to develop an ethic for their public lives which leaves them free to pursue in private their own particular religious or other moralities. … Medicine, at least in the West, is a secular profession practiced in a pluralist society." (FB: The need to lead this double life may be a reason for the prevalence of psychiatric disturbances among doctors.)

—ROSS KESSEL, *The Lancet*, April 25, 1992

MENTAL HEALTH

In 1999 Dr. Berger said, "We need new breakthroughs in treatment." Research in neuropsychiatry since then has yielded major changes in diagnosis and treatment of mental illness, but his views remain of interest.

Mental health, or psychological maturity, is having the ability to work and the capacity to love. Mental disturbance is exhibited by irrational behavior and inadequate performance.

Mentally disturbed, i.e. insane, people are different from emotionally disturbed psychopaths. Mentally disturbed patients have difficulty distinguishing between the real and the imaginary and differentiating between important and unimportant problems. Psychopaths have no sense of responsibility nor do they have a conscience—they enjoy cruelty. They have an emotional disturbance.

Not all mental disturbances are real. Some are affectations, often clinician-enhanced or copycat syndromes. Sometimes mental illness is a label that mainstream society pins on eccentrics. The anatomical and biochemical changes observed in psychiatric patients may also be just part of a syndrome but not the cause. The only symptom of a mental disturbance may be seen in functional impairment—being unable to perform the tasks of daily living.

Delusions, for instance, are implausible beliefs that are firmly held, idiosyncratic, and utterly lacking in social validation. A psychiatric delusion is a fixed, dominating, or persistent false mental conception resistant to reason with regard to actual things or matters of fact. A mental disturbance in essence is an inability or unwillingness to use reason.

Damaging Ideas

Many of our problems in life arise from our self-injurious behavior patterns, our inappropriate and self-damaging lifestyles. Yet we stubbornly cling to what are clearly self-harming tendencies, attitudes, and ingrained habits. These self-damaging ideas can give rise to inappropriate mental responses and ruinous behavior patterns.

Distorted or wrongly valued ideas, ideals, or mindsets can and do cause discomfort and malfunction of the mind. The nagging presence of such generalized psychic pain can produce the flight to and dependence upon addictions to alcohol and other drugs. Identification with rigid and unreal religious or patriotic beliefs can also block the ability to accept self-correcting information from the real world. Stress, anger, and anxiety result from this conflict between psychological appearances and factual reality. Psychosomatic pain is a reaction to anger and stress.

Freud believed it was caused by traumatic childhood events. But most of us had such experiences during childhood without suffering from mental illness later, so psychoneurotic and psychiatric symptoms are not necessarily the result of insults, trauma, and pain suffered in childhood. Instead, many of these symptoms are due to a lack of knowledge about how to handle the problems of living. Other contributing factors are one's genetic makeup or an unfriendly social environment. For instance, we all need continuous mental stimulation. Those cared for in environments that lack this stimulation may deteriorate into disturbance.

Treatment

There is one set of problems common to all, or almost all, who come to psychotherapy: a) a sense of helplessness; b) a fear of being unable to cope; c) a conviction that change is not possible. What psychotherapy can do is a) teach people to react appropriately to their problems and b) help them find relief from their sense of impotence.

To help people, one has to understand their primary world of meaning. In a paper given to the Royal Medical Society in London, May 14, 1985, psychiatrist J. D. Frank said our "thinking, feeling and behavior are responses to the meanings of events as much as to the events themselves. We are guided largely by our assumptions about reality, and the distress and disability of our patients are determined by how they construe their experiences." Though patients may be unable to change their experiences, we can "transform the meanings of their experiences in such a way as to enable them to feel better and function more effectively … replacing confusion with clarity."

To assess the intentions of a person and to understand his behavior, one must focus not only on his overt actions but also on what he does not do or say, because that can be just as significant, or more so. The absences are better noted and remembered when labeled in a concrete, active way: someone who is sexually unresponsive is considered frigid; one who lacks enthusiasm is called gloomy and apathetic.

Neurosis does not "befall one" but instead is created and arranged and protected. Madness relieves one of responsibility.

The really crucial insights are those that are closely linked to new actions. To be useful, these insights must be transforming: it is important for the patient not only to understand but also to act differently.

People will put out what is expected of them. To envision excellence is to encourage it, and to anticipate failure is to promote it.

❧

"The Common Health cannot be considered properly apart from the Common Happiness. I propose … a particular aspect of mind, the

Quiet Mind … as the highest product of mental hygiene. It is a quality in the mind which balances intelligence with energy and gentleness with fortitude. Its foundation is integrity. On this foundation a diligent search for, and a strict adherence to, Truth build the house. The coping stone is control."

—LORD HORDER (1871–1955), *The Lancet*, April 2, 1938

"Treat a man as he is and he will remain as he is. Treat a man as he can and should be and he will become as he can and should be."

—GOETHE (1749–1832)

"Frustration of an instinct—the damming up of the spirit—can make us sick. The damming up of a vital impulse."

—CARL GUSTAV JUNG (1875–1961), in Michael Grosso,
The Final Choice (Stillpoint, 1985)

Drugs v. Psychotherapy

Psychoactive drugs have shown that it is possible to find effective remedies even if the nature of the illness is not completely understood. These new drugs are also of value as tools to help us elucidate the biochemical roots of disturbed behavior. They can help us find still more effective means to combat and eradicate the mental diseases that cause such unhappiness and deprive us of intellect and dignity.

As a rule, however, psychiatric treatments do not counteract all clinical manifestations of a mental disorder. While antipsychotic drugs may suppress paranoid ideation, for instance, they leave affective withdrawal unaffected. They are also highly effective in suppressing manic behavior in bipolar depression.

Psychiatric drugs, in contrast to antidiabetics and antihypertensives, are observed to be effective only in some patients suffering from a specific disorder. This and the fact that electro-convulsive treatments appear to be effective for several mental disorders quite distinct from one another, such as major depression, catatonia, and aggression, indicates to me that there is something wrong with our classification of mental disorders.

There are misunderstandings about tranquilizers, about what they can and cannot do, who should use them, when and why to use them. They may make you feel normal again, able to cope again, but are no substitute for philosophy.

A disease of the mind cannot be cured with chemicals alone; attitudes must also change. Psychoanalysis and other psychodynamic procedures often succeed, as Freud said they should, in "transforming neurotic suffering into everyday unhappiness."

A fundamental assumption of psychoanalysis is that our mental processes are continuous: they continue during sleep and other states of altered consciousness. Our mental lives are split between conscious and unconscious states, over which we have no control. The kind of rationality presupposed in the idea of human beings being free is accordingly invalidated. It is often difficult to act rationally because our behavior is so influenced by the subconscious we do not control.

"Therapeutic neutrality" is positive and caring regard, but only if honest. By asking questions but giving no answers, you never discount the other person's viewpoint and never back away from your own. This honors patients by letting them find their own answers. But be unwilling to participate in a power struggle. When you come to a confrontation, you have already lost. The confrontation itself means that neutrality has been replaced with judgment.

Ultimately, it is not possible to motivate another person. The best one can do is create an atmosphere and opportunity for the person to motivate himself. Remind the patient, through questions rather than statements or advice, to remember his purpose in life, and explain how he could help himself. This was expressed by poet Guillaume Apollinaire (1880–1918): "'Come to the edge,' he said. They said, 'We are afraid.' 'Come to the edge,' he said. They came. He pushed them— and they flew."

Intensive psychotherapy is sometimes needed to help the patient accept the need for chronic medication. In *An Unquiet Mind: A Memoir of Moods and Madness* (Knopf, 1995), K R. Jamison (1946–) wrote, "No pill can help me deal with the problem of not wanting to take pills; likewise no amount of psychotherapy alone can prevent my manias and depressions. I need both."

࿔

"American society has adopted the ethics of psychoanalysis as its creed—that one's actions should be geared to satisfying oneself without undue regard for the feeling of others."
—ROBERT BELLAH (1927–2013), *Habits of the Heart*
(University of California Press, 1985)

"Neurotransmitters are the key to therapy for virtually all mental diseases which result from communication failures at the chemical level."
—LEROY HOOD (1938–), University of Washington, Seattle

"Psychoanalysts believe that [patients'] insight into their difficulties is the crucial factor in deep and lasting therapeutic change. Not necessarily so, e.g., fear of elevators. The insight into the difficulties of these patients can be achieved without any apparent reduction in their miseries. What may be curative in analysis is primarily the experience of being understood rather than any particular understanding that may be achieved."

—HEINZ KOHUT (1913–1981)

Trends in Psychology

- *Behaviorism:* A research trend beginning in the early eighteenth century. In experimental psychology, its aim was to eliminate from discussion any reference to an animal's internal state or subjective experience.
- *Darwinism:* The theory of evolution is not limited to the structural features of organisms, noted Darwin (1809–1882). "The difference in mind between man and the higher animals, great as it is, certainly is one of degree and not of kind."
- *Dualism:* Although psychology is now often defined as the study of behavior, it is nonetheless clear that its arrival helped legitimize dualism (mind v. body), and that psychology remains the principle vehicle for dualistic ideas among the scientific disciplines.
- *Existentialism:* The human subject must be the focus. Existence of myself as a free agent precedes and has priority over any absolute external values because the only thing I can know for certain is what I think and feel, and that I am conscious and outside the causal rule of objects. Determined neither by the past (Freud) or by social conditions (Marx), I alone give meaning to my world. My anguish and loneliness result from my total freedom. I live in a world of my own choosing and am free to escape.

- The *Freudian* notion: Our mental lives are split between conscious and unconscious states, over which we have no control. In this view, it is difficult to act rationally because our behavior is so greatly influenced by our uncontrollable subconscious.
- *Gestalt* therapy: The central tenet is that the whole is different from the sum of its parts.
- *Holistic Health*: According to holistic practice, the body, mind, and spirit have to be treated together as a whole. The key lesson of the holistic model is "sing your own song"—do what gives you satisfaction and discard everything that makes you unhappy.
- *Maslow's Humanist Model* (Abraham Maslow, 1908–1970): This aimed to help people achieve their potential for self-growth and self-fulfillment. Its weak spot is the belief that everybody is born good and will stay good. But people are not innately good or bad but are shaped by their social environment and upbringing.
- *The Marxist Model*: Here the real basis for all activities and ideas is the economic structure of society, and most struggles in history are seen as between classes. The state is the mechanism whereby the dominant class forcibly maintains its rule over the others, controlling the raw materials and means of production. The most important beliefs in society will serve primarily to protect the power of this ruling class.
- *Mentalism:* This theory presupposes a dichotomy between the physical and spiritual realms, the latter of which is identified with subjective experience.
- *The Science of Human Action*: Ludwig von Mises (1881–1973), the Austrian economist and philosopher, explained economic and sociological events through the actions of individuals. His premise was that individuals strive to improve their own well-being.

MONEY, WEALTH, BEING RICH

Cash is freedom. First and foremost, it's a way to be in a position to act when one really wants to act. Freedom demands that you do something with it.

The rich man does not continue to make more money because he needs it but because he has to maintain his self-respect.

We must make money so that we have the time and leisure to do more important things. If you are rich and do not have to work anymore, your real job is not to make more money but to figure out what you ought to achieve with it.

Gambling is when you bet on something and cannot afford to lose.

The only inflation hedge there is in the world is to make money.

There is nothing wrong with being rich as long as one becomes rich doing things that are more important than being rich.

ॐ

"Money:
- is like muck. Not good except it be spread."—FRANCIS BACON (1561–1626)
- hides a thousand imperfections."—CHINESE PROVERB
- is coined liberty."—DOSTOEVSKY (1821–1861)
- doesn't bring happiness, but it calms the nerves."—FRENCH PROVERB

"I have always found it curious that the two things a human being must cope with all his life, his body and his money, are never explained to him at school. Few adults ever know where their liver is until too late, and few ever know where their money is—until the savings and loan system collapses."

GORE VIDAL (1925–2012), quoted by John Simon in
The American Spectator, January 1993

"The law of human beings is wisdom and goodness, not unlimited acquisition."

—ROBERT M. HUTCHINS (1899–1977)

"If seeking wealth were a decent pursuit, I too would seek it, even if I had to work as a janitor. As it is, I'd rather follow my inclinations."

—CONFUCIUS (551–479 BCE), *Analects,* tr. Simon Leys (Norton, 1997)

"Everything comes to him who does not want."

—SIR HERBERT BEERBOHM TREE (1852–1917)

"There is no more fatal blunderer than he who consumes the greater part of his life getting his living."

—HENRY DAVID THOREAU (1817–1862)

"One of the first arts of life is to have no delicacy about money."

—GEORGE BERNARD SHAW (1856–1950),
Letter to Molly Tompkins, 1920s

"A large income is the best recipe for happiness I ever heard of."

—JANE AUSTEN (1775–1817), *Mansfield Park*

"When it is a question of money, everyone is of the same religion."
—Voltaire (1694–1778)

"You are fortunate when you can afford to be virtuous."
—Malcolm Forbes (1919–1990)

N

NATURE v. MAN-MADE

Natural is what comes from nature, what existed before man invented science and started interfering with the environment. Natural and good are not synonymous. Many things that are natural, i.e., that occur spontaneously in nature and are not due to the interference of man, are bad, undesirable, and destructive. Examples include earthquakes, floods, and other natural catastrophes, cancer and all other diseases. So although we are surrounded by misery, pain, and injustice, not all of this is man-made or due to man's inhumanity to man. Much of it is caused by Mother Nature.

The saying "Nature knows best" implies that man-made things are inferior. That just is not so. What is wrong with art, or for that matter with airplanes, locomotives, or modern medicine? All these are made by man.

&

"The order of nature is so imperfect as to require incessant amendment by man."
—AUGUSTE COMTE (1798–1857)

"If the artificial is not better than the natural, to what end are all the arts of life? To dig, to plow, to build, to wear clothes are direct infringements on the injunction to follow nature. … In sober truth, nearly all the things which men are hanged or imprisoned for doing to one another, are nature's everyday performances. The duty of man is the same in respect to his own nature of all other things, namely not to follow but to amend it. Conformity to nature has no connection whatever with right or wrong."

—John Stuart Mill (1806–1873), *On Nature*

"McHughen successfully demonstrates the senselessness of thinking that the more natural something is, the better it is for you. If a nation wants to protect the environment and the health of people and animals alike, it will often have to tamper with nature. ... Mill was right to say that 'the duty of man is not to follow nature but to amend it.'"

—Cass R. Sunstein (1954–) reviewing Alan McHughen's
*Pandora's Basket: The Potential Hazards of
Genetically Modified Foods, TNR,* October 23, 2000

P

PAST, FUTURE, MEMORY

If we could predict the future, it would mean what is to come has been ordained and cannot be changed. Our inability to do so actually means we have enormous power to shape what will come. We can also monitor it as it emerges. Science permits us to do that with increasing perceptiveness and accuracy.

For many people, dissatisfaction with the modern world comes not from the need for something more, but from a futile wish to go back to some earlier, supposedly less complex order. We spend a lot of time thinking about what went wrong, but progress is only possible if we stop singing praises to the good old times, which were not necessarily so wonderful. They were rife with hunger, sickness, wars, oppression, and persecution.

The world finds it difficult to adjust to the two great advances of the past thirty or forty years. These are, first, our increased understanding of the way the universe works and, second, our ability to receive information and communicate by the printed word, through radio, television, and the Internet. The impact of these two dimensions is profound and unnerving. And, indeed, the central intellectual principle of the new age and of progress is doubt.

❧

"If you want to predict the future, create it."

—PETER DRUCKER (1909–2005)

"By defining the past, memory creates the present. ... Man is his memory. Those who suffer memory loss don't just misplace their keys, they lose themselves. They become lost and adrift in time, because without memory the current moment has no context and no meaning."
—Rabbi Nachum Braverman, *Olam*, Winter 2001

"What we search for does not exist until we find it. ... The past empowers the present, and the groping footsteps leading to this present mark the pathways to the future."
—Mary Catherine Bateson (1939–), *Composing a Life—*
A Work in Progress (Plume, 1989)

"Humans have so far been interested mainly in their own private roots, and have therefore never claimed the whole of the inheritance into which they are born, the legacy of everybody's past experience. Each generation searches only for what it thinks it lacks, and recognizes only what it knows already."
—Theodore Zeldin (1933–), *An Intimate History of Humanity*
(Harper Perennial, 1995)

"The difficulty lies not in new ideas, but in escaping from old ones."
—J. M. Keynes (1883–1946), *General Theory of Employment,*
Interest and Money (Cambridge University Press, 1936)

"The past is the present, but older."
Alan Abelson (1925–2013), *Barron's,* July 17, 1995

PERCEPTION AND BELIEFS

Our state of mind and our behavior are largely determined not by what we know, by our abilities or the truth—i.e., the facts—but by our beliefs.

What one perceives—and what one does not—are also functions of one's beliefs and desires.

While the facts are fixed, the frame of mind in which we choose to perceive and interpret them can make the difference between hope and despair, optimism and pessimism.

What seems absurd to us reflects our previous experience and conclusions. Many of the most fundamental claims of science are the antithesis of common sense and appear absurd on their face. The great contribution of Einstein's equation on the equivalence of mass and energy, for example, is that the fundamental building blocks that make up everything in the universe, including the human body, are invisible particles. The particles are a combination of mass and energy, are smaller than an atom or a proton and possibly smaller than a quark.

Consider Richard Lewontin (1929–), in a review of *The Demon-Haunted World* by Carl Sagan (*NYR*, January 9, 1997): "Do physicists really expect me to accept without serious qualms that the pungent cheese I had for lunch is really made up of tiny tasteless, odorless, colorless packets of energy with nothing but empty space between them? … Our willingness to accept scientific claims that are against common sense is the key to an understanding of the real struggle between science and the supernatural. We take the side of science … because we have a prior commitment, a commitment to materialism." Copyright © 1997 by Richard Lewontin

Or John Horgan's (1953–) description of Newton's discovery (in *The Sciences*, May/June 1996): "Newton's formalism for gravity … smacked of the occult to his contemporaries. How can one thing possibly tug at another across vast distances of empty space? … self-evident preposterousness. … But the important thing is that the formalism works; its truth is not threatened by mere weirdness."

❧

"Ideas do not come to power because they are truths. Ideas come to power because they are beliefs. And the popularity of a belief has nothing to do with its truth."

—LEON WIESELTIER (1952–), *TNR*, May 15, 1995

"Everything depends on the observer's frame of reference. What you see depends on your point of view."

—ALBERT EINSTEIN (1879–1955)

"People are disturbed not by things but by the view they take of them."

—EPICTETUS (55–135)

"There are no facts, only interpretations."

—FRIEDRICH NIETZSCHE (1844–1900)

"We do not know what is. All we know is what we perceive. The physical phenomena are shaped in fundamental ways by our perception of them."

—NIELS BOHR (1885–1962), 1932

"What is it humans really fear? The absolute strength of the threat is not as important as its relative value. It does not matter so much what a person can objectively lose; the absolute value of the threat is never as important as the subjective meaning it has for him. There is nobody who has not something he does not want to lose; everybody has something to lose and everybody has cause for anxiety."

—VACLAV HAVEL (1936–2011)

PERSONALITY, CHARACTER

The difference between character and personality is that by character we mean an individual's moral constitution and by personality his mental, emotional, and social characteristics.

The hardest test of human character is this: Do you change out of recognition when your circumstances do? Why do we over- or under-tip a waiter in a place we will never see again? Because our behavior affects how we feel about ourselves. The decision to tip in a distant city is in part a decision about the character traits we wish to cultivate.

There are many different aspects to each personality. Look at the sides of Dostoevsky described by Stanislaw Baranczak (*TNR*, May 15, 1995). Dostoevsky was no liberal: he was a monarchist and Great Russian imperialist who idolized the czar. He despised anything German or Swiss and believed that these countries lagged behind the Russian Empire. He had a special hatred for the "Polacks," which was nothing less than "a hatred for the downtrodden. ... This prejudice is surprising in a writer ... who had enough Christian compassion and human understanding to create subtle and touching portrayals of prostitutes, down-and-out drunkards and even murderers."

In 1950 David Riesman proposed, in his *The Lonely Crowd*, two types of personality that reflected character: the inner-directed and the other-directed. Martin Peretz quoted Arthur Schlesinger, Jr.'s (1917–2007) views of these in *TNR*, August 4, 2000: "The inner-directed's ... values and purposes are implanted within. [The] other-directed ... takes his standards from the group in which he aspires to live, and realizes himself as he identifies what he deems respectable and enviable in the world outside himself." The inner-directed person "feels guilty when he violates his inner ideals.... The other-directed has no inner ideals to violate."

John Ruskin (1819–1900) connected character to "taste": "It is just the vital function of all our being. What we *like* determines what we *are*, and is the sign of what we are; and to teach taste is inevitably to form character."

❧

"A four-component model of temperament developed by C. R. Cloninger, MD (1944–): novelty-seeking, avoidance of harm, reward dependence, persistence."
—STEPHEN JAY GOULD (1941–2002), cited in Natural History,
March 1998

"Habits constitute the self, they are will, they form our effective desires and they rule our thought. Character is the interpretation of these habits, seeking to bring competing tendencies into unity."
—JOHN DEWEY (1859–1952)

"A moral character cannot be created by argument, 'education,' or an act of will. It cannot be created by any kind of planned action, whether scientific, moral or religious. Like true love, it is a gift, not an achievement. It depends on accidents such as parental affection, some kind of stability, friendship, and—following therefrom—on a delicate balance between self-confidence and concern for others."
—PAUL FEYERABEND (1924–1994), quoted by Richard Rorty from Killing
Time: The Autobiography of Paul Feyerabend, TNR, July 31, 1995

Clark M. Clifford (1906–1998), adviser to four U.S. presidents, ended a presentation at the Cosmos Club in Washington on October 16, 1986, by answering the question: Is there any one lesson you have learned from this unique experience? He quoted a brief statement by Horace

Greeley (1811–1872), an outstanding nineteenth-century newspaper editor: "Fame is a vapor, popularity is an accident, riches take wings, those who cheer today may curse tomorrow and only one thing endures: character."

"If one disdains the low and the near, and restlessly seeks the high and the far, skips over the steps and crosses the limits, one will be drifting in emptiness and vacuity, without anything to rely on."

—LU TSU-CHIEN, 1176

PHILOSOPHY

Dylan Thomas once wrote about how disappointed he was as a child when someone gave him a book about the wasp, "which told me everything about it except why." The one thing we really want to know is why. Science teaches us to find out how but not to ask why, so there are many answers we don't know. The only discipline that attempts to answer why is philosophy, so we cannot afford to be without it. The goal of philosophy is to assist us in understanding ourselves.

Science is concerned with the gathering of facts. Philosophy is concerned with more abstract matters, including 1) critical assessment of arguments; 2) formulation and testing of principles; 3) analysis of concepts.

Definitions and Descriptions

The basic questions of philosophy include: Can physical reality be taken to exist independently of ourselves? Is the world affected by the way we choose to look at it—by our conscious perception of the nature of reality, and by our apparent free will?

But philosophy is not merely an analysis of ideas; it is also an expression of basic life choices and interpretations. Instead of trying to find out how to make this the good life, philosophy is preoccupied with many subjects that either cannot increase our satisfaction with life, or that attempt to find answers to questions that cannot be answered.

We need philosophers because it is hard to tell which beliefs are essential to liberal democracy and which are petrified and tyrannical dogmas. Telling the difference is the job of philosophers. Rummaging through common sense, trying to figure out what to keep and what to throw away, is what they do.

If the task of philosophy were to find answers to the problems of living, the history of Western philosophy would be one of brilliant failures of philosophical systems that were unable to solve these problems. Instead, the tasks of philosophy are to increase our understanding and insights and permit us to deal with problems that are not yet accessible to the exact sciences.

Philosophers write learned treatises about the disastrous mistakes made by other philosophers instead of sticking with the immutable human rights and moral responsibilities as defined in classic philosophy. Most people would like to know what these are, if, indeed, they exist, without learning all about the mistakes of philosophers.

Philosophy should not be a set of doctrines. It should be a way of life. To address our problems we have to stay clear-headed, sober, and skeptical. We have to know what words and actions really mean. We have to know that miracles do not happen.

Philosophical thought, understanding, and insight on the one hand and success in everyday life on the other should not be mutually exclusive; they should interact and be mutually enhancing.

❧

"The perennial task of philosophers is to examine whatever seems insusceptible to the methods of the sciences or everyday observation."

—ISAIAH BERLIN (1909–1997), *The Times* (of London), November 6, 1998

"The attempt to push rational inquiry obstinately to its limits is bound often to fail, and when the attempt fails, the dream of reason that motivates philosophical thinking seems merely a mirage." (FB: However, when it succeeds it becomes science—and ceases to be called philosophy.)

—ANTHONY GOTTLIEB, *The Dream of Reason* (Norton, 2000)

"By enlarging the objects of [man's] thoughts, [philosophy] supplies an antidote to the anxieties and anguish of the present, and makes possible the nearest approach to serenity that is available to a sensitive mind in our tortured and uncertain world."

—BERTRAND RUSSELL (1872–1970), *Unpopular Essays* (Simon & Schuster, 1950)

"The object of philosophy is the logical clarification of thoughts. Philosophy is not a theory but an activity. The result of philosophy is not a number of 'philosophical propositions' but to make propositions clear."

—LUDWIG WITTGENSTEIN (1889–1951)

"These are the questions that philosophy attempts to answer: Does life have meaning? Are there objective ethical truths? Do we have free will? What is the nature of our identity as selves? Must our knowledge and understanding stay within fixed limits?"

—ROBERT NOZICK (1938–2002), *Philosophical Explanations* (Belknap Press, 1981)

"The first step toward philosophy is incredulity. Father, the truth is, there are no laws for the wise man."

—DENIS DIDEROT (1713–1784)

"You philosophers are sages in your maxims and fools in your conduct."

—BENJAMIN FRANKLIN (1706–1790)

"Philosophical wisdom we parade not in our dress but in our hearts, grandeur we show not in our speech but in our lives."

— MARCUS MINUCIUS FELIX (ca. 160–250), *The Octavius,*
tr. G. W. Clarke (Paulist Press, 1974)

"What we know is what we can perceive through our senses. Gods have no concern for men. … Vain is the word of a philosopher by which no mortal suffering is healed. Just as medicine confers no benefit if it does not drive away bodily disease, so is philosophy useless if it does not drive away the suffering of the mind."

—EPICURUS (341–269 BCE), *On Philosophy*

"*La théorie c'est bon, mais ça n'empêche pas d'exister.*" (Theory is all very well, but it does not prevent facts from existing.)

—JEAN-MARTIN CHARCOT (1825–1893)

Philosophers and Philosophies

Metaphysics (i.e., speculative philosophy) is concerned with abstract thoughts or subjects such as existence, causality, truth, and the transcending of what is directly accessible to experience.

Ontology is the study of the nature of reality; epistemology is the study of the nature of knowledge.

The two animating spirits of the Enlightenment were skepticism—all ideas must face scrutiny—and regard for the individual, which leads to tolerance.

Many new philosophical thoughts, such as "social constructivism" or "deconstructionism," do not increase our understanding of life and the universe. They hide behind a ponderous and impenetrable argot.

According to Plato (427–347 BCE), there are three levels on which people operate, both as individuals and as members of a society or state: 1) Reason, the highest level, searches for truth and virtue. In the state it is represented by the guardians. 2) The spirited elements, the second level, consists of emotions like love, hate, and anger. They are concerned with honor and are represented on the state level by the warriors. 3) The bodily appetites, the lowest level, are concerned with hunger, sex, the attainment of money, and prestige. On the state level, they are represented by the producers.

Plato is a political absolutist. He demands subordination of the individual to the state.

There are two things Plato has not solved: 1) He believes in absolute values. Are there any? 2) He says that government is justified by knowledge of justice, but are there unchanging forms of justice? Who guards the guardians?

The philosophy of Friedrich Nietzsche (1844–1900) includes the following:
1) God is dead.
2) Religion is a trick of tyrants to keep the masses subdued.
3) Democracy is a scheme for keeping the superior few under the power of the inferior many.

John Dewey (1859–1952) saw philosophy not as an academic exercise but rather as the means of solving political and social problems and meeting the needs of people. For Dewey, all value judgments are penultimate. We have to justify and evaluate the outcomes of some courses of conduct as more valid (or valuable) than others. These judgments have to be made on rational grounds. There are no inevitable laws of social development. What will occur depends on us.

Adapted from "The Philosophy of John Dewey" in *Free Inquiry*, Winter 1992–93:

- Any activity pursued on behalf of an ideal is religious in quality.
- Religion should unite people by a set of shared ideals about better social institutions, community spirit, and a sense of personal concern.
- Religion should be decoupled from supernatural goals such as a longing for eternal life. There is no need to worry about things we cannot understand or change.
- Education should match the capacities and interests of children.
- *At the heart of all policy is a value judgment.* (FB italics.) No important problem in human affairs is merely or purely technical.
- Empirical thinkers from Hume to Russell believed that there could be no rational grounds for the choice of ultimate values.

A. J. Ayer (1910–1989): "Logical Positivism"—best defined as against religion and traditional metaphysics, and for empirical science. Many philosophical problems are not to be solved by acquiring more information. What is needed is that we succeed in obtaining a clearer view of what the problems involve.

Heinz von Foerster (1911–2002): We need to ask not what language is, but how it emerged: "I see the problem of language very much the same as the problem of the navel. Ontologically the navel makes no sense. ...

Ontogenetically, however, we see that it is a necessity. We would not be here without it. ... When you don't see how things become, you may not see how things are." From *Dream of Reality: Heinz von Foerster's Constructivisim* by Lynn Segal (Springer, 2001).

According to the *Essentialism* of Karl Popper (1902–1994), the surest path to intellectual perdition is the abandonment of real problems for the sake of verbal problems. What matters is formulation of problems.

Ludwig Wittgenstein (1889–1951):
- Not how the world is, is mystical, but that it is.
- The limits of my language are the limits of my world. We cannot think what we cannot say.
- Philosophy is a battle against the bewitchment of our intelligence by means of language.
- Philosophical work consists of dismantling confusions and mythologies by paying careful attention to our ordinary concepts. Everything that can be said can be said clearly.
- Say what you choose, so long as it does not prevent you from seeing the facts.
- His aim in philosophy? "To show the fly the way out of the fly-bottle." To teach you to pass from a piece of disguised nonsense to something that is patent nonsense.
- Whereof one cannot speak, thereof one must be silent. (The last sentence of his *Tractatus Logico-Philosophicus*)

❦

"The question why there are beings (things) rather than nothing is the fundamental theosophical question. Anyone for whom the Bible contains a divine revelation has the final answer to this question before it is asked, explicitly everything that is, except for God himself, has been created by God, and God himself is the uncreated creator. Thus anyone who holds such faith can in no way genuinely participate in the asking of the fundamental philosophical problems, for if he asks the question seriously, he ceases to be a genuine believer."

—MARTIN HEIDEGGER (1889–1976)

Metaphysics "does not move mountains and it will not save the world. It cannot cure the common cold or put bread on the table. But those are not all the things that a human life demands."

—PETER BERKOWITZ (1959–), *TNR*, April 7, 1997

"Enlightenment is man's exodus from his self-incurred tutelage. Tutelage is the inability to use one's understanding without the guidance of another person. This tutelage is self-incurred if its cause lies not in any weakness of understanding, but in indecision and lack of courage to use the mind without the guidance of another. Dare to know (*sapere aude*). Have the courage to use your own understanding. This is the motto of the Enlightenment."

—IMMANUEL KANT (1724–1804), *Critique of Pure Reason*

"My philosophy, in essence, is the concept of man as a heroic being, with his own happiness as the moral purpose of his life, with productive achievement as his noblest activity, and reason as his only absolute."

—AYN RAND (1905–1982)

"Nihilism for Nietzsche (1844–1900) was not the end but the beginning, of wisdom. The 'Übermensch' is not a higher race. It is Man himself—once he learns to affirm who he really is. We are to celebrate what we are and what we have always been: the creators of value. We must not subject ourselves to some supposedly pre-given values: 'We have art that we may not perish of truth.' In contrast, Plato believes

that the objective world contains not just matter and mind, but value too. Some values exist independently of our will."
—STEVEN E. ASCHEIM (1942–), *The Nietzsche Legacy in Germany 1890–1990* (University of California Press, 1994)

Karl Popper (1904–1994) wrote:
- Philosophy should be concerned with genuine problems—and not just linguistic puzzles ... our often unconscious views on the theory of knowledge and its central problems ("What can we know?" "How certain is our knowledge?") are decisive for our attitude toward ourselves and toward politics.
- The essence of a rational or reasonable attitude is an openness to criticism, readiness to be criticized, and eagerness to criticize oneself. Implicit in this attitude is the realization that we shall always have to live in an imperfect society. This is so because even very good people are imperfect because we do not know enough and because there always exist irresolvable clashes of values.
- There are many moral problems which are insoluble because moral principles conflict.
- The fact that moral values or principles may clash does not invalidate them. This does not mean, however, that any set of values can be defended (relativism).
- There is no better synonym for "rational" than "critical." Belief, of course, is never rational: it is rational to suspend belief.
- All nationalism or racialism is evil, and Jewish nationalism is no exception.
- For I believe that there is only one excuse for a lecture: to challenge. But in matters of the intellect (as opposed, perhaps, to art, or to politics) nothing is less creative and more commonplace than conservatism.
- [W]e should not be swayed by our theories to give up common sense too easily.

- Explanation is always incomplete: we can always raise another why question.

- Essentialism: the view that there are ideas or essences in the nature of things binding both for our ideas and our morals. (This is the heart of Platonism.)

- By an objective theory, I mean a theory that is arguable, which can be exposed to rational criticism, preferably a theory that can be tested; not one which merely appeals to our subjective intuitions.

- Metaphysical realism—the view that there is a real world to be discovered. The theory of natural selection is not a testable scientific theory but a metaphysical research program.

- *Naturphilosophie* is an attempt to invoke Nature and History to underwrite and vindicate our values, and to be the guarantor of our destiny. We must stand up like free men and choose our values.

- Truth exists and the purpose of science is to strive to reach it. There is no final authority for deciding truth.*

(FB: Popper's three most important theories are:

1) History has no eternal or unchanging laws. It devours everything and will devour Communism as well.

2) The most important criterion for categorizing societies and individuals is their degree of openness to other cultures, to their principles and values. An open society is one that accepts the Other and is ready to acknowledge that Other's opinions and choices. The closed attitude toward the Other characterizes the three plagues of the contemporary world—nationalism, racism, and religious fundamentalism.

---

* Reprinted by permission of Open Court Publishing Company, a division of Carus Publishing Company, dba ePals Media, Chicago IL, from *The Philosophy of Karl Popper* edited by Paul A. Schilpp (Library of Living Philosophers Volume XIV), copyright © 1974 by Open Court.

3) Ignorance is not a simple lack of knowledge but an active aversion to knowledge, the refusal to know issuing from cowardice, pride, or laziness of mind. Ignorance has an ethical dimension, and knowing is a moral obligation for human beings.)

THE POOR

The opponents of an open society want, among other things, to transfer power to the private sector and abolish all government control and interference. They conveniently forget all the abuses of the past and propose to take care of the poor and helpless by charity. They forget that charity, as George Bernard Shaw (1856-1950) has stressed, will never eradicate poverty. It merely eases the bad conscience of the benefactor and humiliates the recipient.

Is welfare responsible for the moral decay of our society? If so, we have to eliminate charitable gifts, as they are a form of welfare. Charity treats the symptoms, not the disease, and gratitude implies not only appreciation but also obligation and indebtedness.

The growing gap between the rich and the poor is an important social problem. The poor have to be trained and educated. This is not done—funds for it are not made available by Congress.

છે

"Kant (1724–1804) believed that all human beings are born with equal and inalienable rights. Accordingly, his view on charity: 'What properly belongs to me must not be accorded to me as something I beg for.

The problem with private benevolence as with public charity is that it treats its objects as pitiable, as beggars, and this is a way of refusing to recognize their rights. It conceals our own injustice.'"
—SIMON BLACKBURN (1944–), reviewing *Kant: A Biography* by Manfred Kuehn, *TNR*, April 16, 2001

"Poverty results more from injustice than from personal characteristics or bad luck. ... The collective wealth of the middle and upper classes is necessarily built on the collective deprivation of the poor. ... Every person has worth and value despite external circumstances ... some variant of 'managed competition' combining free market forces with government regulation will [not] solve the nation's health problems."
—DAVID HILFIKER, MD (1945–), *Not All of Us Are Saints* (Hill & Wang, 2004)

"We—the middle classes, I mean, not merely the very rich—have neglected you. Instead of justice we have offered you charity, and instead of sympathy we have offered you hard and unreal advice."
—ARNOLD TOYNBEE (1889–1975)

"Public Assistance and the Welfare State: The purpose of the welfare state is to preserve equalities of respect in the face of inequalities of luck, talent, income and wealth. Public assistance provides help to those who need it without demeaning or humiliating the recipient."
—RICHARD SENNETT (1943–), *Respect in a World of Inequality* (Norton, 2004)

"Being unwanted is the worst disease that any human being can ever experience."
—MOTHER THERESA (1910–1997)

"There can be no armistice in our struggle against suffering."
—VICTOR BROMBERT, *NYT*, August 22, 1975

R

RACISM, PREJUDICE, TOLERANCE

Racism and ethnic prejudice see a part stand as the whole. The hater hates them all: the dead, the unborn, and all he has not met.

Racists and anti-Semites believe that nonwhites and Jews are responsible for the world's troubles and must be eliminated.

If racism is wrong, all religions are wrong too, because both are based on an unproven belief or a revealed truth.

The potential achievement of a racial group is expressed by the highest attainment achieved by a member of the group; it cannot be assessed by measuring its statistical averages of achievement.

Silence gives consent to bigotry.

Tolerance merely requires minimal respect. You do not have to like another person, or even respect him as an individual. You just have to be willing to live and let live—respect the right of other human beings to live their lives their own way—whether you like it or not.

What matters is to treat with respect those people with whom you profoundly disagree. Open disagreement is a higher form of respect than tolerance because it means you take their beliefs seriously enough to oppose them and defend your own. To say that all beliefs are equally deserving of tolerance is to admit that they are all equally unimportant.

Although the idea that every point of view has to be tolerated as long as nobody is seriously injured is not acceptable, neither are ideas that push people to be intolerant of others.

ॐ

"This universal tolerance for ideas—both reasonable and unreasonable—is coupled with a disturbing intolerance for people. The philosophy that sees only 'local' truths rather than universal truths not only repudiates science (the attempt to know the truth) but divides people according to their locality by who, where, when, what color, gender, etc. they are. The natural result of such a division is an intolerance that, in the long run at least, tends to manifest itself in racism, nationalism, sexism and the like."
—GEORGE ENGLEBRETSEN, "Postmodernism and New Age Unreason,"
Genius News 18, June 2002

"Cultural relativism is a fancy name for racism because it justifies two sets of values, rights and privileges for human beings according to a subjective, arbitrary concept, such as 'culture.'"
—AZAR MAJEDI, *New Humanist*

"Knowledge does not guarantee tolerance. Tolerance requires not just knowledge but also virtue. Knowledge and value are not necessarily coextensive. We may or may not value what we know. We may or may not know what we value."
—R. P. VANCE, ET AL., *PBM*, Winter 1992

"Tolerance is the virtue of people who do not believe in anything."
—G. K. CHESTERTON (1874–1936)

"Indifference is the main form of tolerance in the West. Our tolerant attitude is often little more than lack of interest or disbelief; we are as indifferent to our own beliefs as to those of others."
—LESZEK KOLAKOWSKI (1927–2009), quoted by Nathan Gardels,
NPQ, Fall/Winter 2009/2010

"Islam offers the only resistance to the radical indifference sweeping the world."
—JEAN BAUDRILLARD (1929–2007)

"I don't want to be admired for my tolerance. Tolerance is a soft, squishy virtue. Reduced to its lowest common denominator, to tolerate means to abide with repugnance. … Some things are simply too repugnant to abide. When we build up our tolerance level, we become party to other people's crimes. Violence is an intolerable expression of belief. When it comes to violence, or of the inciting of violence, intolerance is the only proper response."
—FORREST CHURCH (1948–2009), Sermon, 1989

"Injustice anywhere is a threat to justice everywhere."
—MARTIN LUTHER KING, JR. (1929–1968)

"But isn't racism wrong regardless of what racists might think? But isn't the sun in the middle of the solar system regardless of what geocentrists might think?"
—DAVID L. HULL (1935–2010), Science, November 12, 1993

"The thread of anti-Polish bias that runs through Dostoevsky's works is harmful to their artistic integrity … because it is based on stereotypical generalization—the sort of logic totally alien to the thinking that otherwise governs his art. The logic of generalization is the reverse side of contempt for the individual."

—STANISLAW BARANCZAK (1946–2014) on Joseph Frank's *Dostoevsky: The Miraculous Years 1865–1871, TNR,* May 15, 1995

"If you wish to understand anti-Semitism, do not study Jews. Study non-Jews, because the fantasies and the atrocities are theirs. If you wish to understand racism, do not study blacks. Study whites, for the same reason. The notion that in some significant sense there are two sides to such questions, that prejudice has a basis in reality and oppression has a cause in the behavior of the oppressed, is itself a concession to the injustice that we despise."

—ADAM MICHNIK (1946–) and LEON WIESELTIER (1952–),
TNR, June 4, 2001

"The bullies and the institutions that tolerate them are the problem. Victims of bullying are not at fault, just as a physically impaired person is not inherently disabled; rather their environment is disabling."

—I. M. CREIGHTON and S. BALEN, Letter to *The Lancet,*
December 15, 2001

"We have made the world we are living in and we have to make it over."

—JAMES BALDWIN (1924–1987), *Nobody Knows My Name*
(Dial Press, 1961)

"Few things have done more harm than the belief on the part of individuals or groups ... that they are in *sole* possession of the truth: especially about how to live, what to be & do—and that those who differ from them ... need restraining or suppressing. ... There are many ways of living, believing, behaving: mere *knowledge* provided by history, anthropology, literature, art, law makes clear that the differences of cultures & characters are as deep as the similarities (which make men human) and that we are none the poorer for this rich variety: knowledge of it opens the windows of the mind (and soul) and makes people wiser, nicer, & more civilized: absence of it breeds irrational prejudice, hatreds, ghastly exterminations ..."

—Isaiah Berlin (1909–1997), *NYR*, October 18, 2001

REALITY AND REASON

What is more "real"—things or ideas we have of things? Does knowledge begin in the senses or in the mind?

Philosophers can prove to their own satisfaction that our mind is the only thing that exists. Even if there is an outside world, it may be totally unlike what you believe it to be. We cannot prove that anything exists outside our minds. The philosophers ask: Is it all right then to go on believing in the external world anyway? This is an irrelevant question. We perceive an external world to exist. Our fate and happiness depend on our getting on in it.

Reality at the present is unknowable. We are aware only of different fragments of reality. What we observe does not necessarily describe it. It just describes what our senses or the machinery at our disposal are able to perceive. For example, we are not aware of the signals sent out by television broadcasting until these are received and converted into signals that our senses can perceive. Moreover, our eye can see only a tiny part of the spectrum of light. Beyond the violet edge there are many other waves that the eye is not able to see: UV, X-rays, and gamma rays. Beyond the red edge are further colors—the infrared that we can feel as heat and the much longer radio wavelength.

"Virtual" is the generation by computer software of an image or environment that appears real to the senses. In virtual reality, nothing is real, but we experience it as if it were.

Our whole sense of what we define as real is connected to a nightlife of thoughts that are strikingly different from the day ones.

"The free man," according to Spinoza, "is one who lives by the dictates of reason alone." Reason is the ability to think and to draw conclusions, to be sane and have good sense, to think logically, i.e., to grasp what is expected by the working of cause and effect. To have a point of view and stand for something on the one hand or to be neutral and nice on the other is not enough. One must 1) obey the dictates of reason, like Spinoza's free man; 2) accept that this is not the best of all possible worlds; and 3) be confident that nobody can hurt you unless you let the person do so, because the reasonable person has freedom of choice.

"Transcendental" means "above reason." There is nothing above reason, but there are worlds where reason does not apply, such as the world of art or feeling. Yet even in these, where reasoning does not control reactivity, we use reason to evaluate. Thus nothing transcends reason.

"Scientific" means valid reasoning from evidence. Boyce Rensberger noted (in *Science,* July 7, 2000) that "pseudoscience ... is based on uncontrolled experiments and anecdotal evidence. ... What makes science special is that evidence has to meet certain standards." Scientific facts are reality, not social constructs. And reality, because of our fallibility, preconceived ideas, environmental factors, and incomplete knowledge, has to be verifiable and repeatable by others to become scientific fact.

❧

"We see the world as nouns and verbs, objects and actions, matter and energy. There may well be other ways of categorizing reality but that is the mode of perception we human beings have been granted and it has been remarkably successful."
> —JOHN HORGAN (1953–), *The Sciences*, May/June 1996

"We cannot meaningfully question the existence of physical objects. It was a mistake to look for some sort of proof of the existence of physical objects."
> —*The Economist*, December 7, 1996

"Humans fear reason, but they ought to fear stupidity—for reason can be hard, but stupidity can be fatal."
> —GOETHE (1749–1832)

"Intellect distinguishes between the possible and the impossible; reason distinguishes between the sensible and the senseless. Even the possible can be senseless."
> —MAX BORN (1882–1970)

"If you are in touch with reality in the sense that you comprehend what is happening around you, and remain cheerful, your high spirits must be either chemically induced or the symptoms of mental impairment."
> —HENRY MILLER (1891–1980), *Sexus* (Grove Press, 1949)

"Life consists of making the best of an inevitable bargain, however hard. Reason is humankind's best hope."
> —JAMES BRYANT CONANT (1893–1978)

"Reality is not the way you wish things to be, nor the way they appear to be, but the way they actually are. ... You either acknowledge reality and use it to your benefit or it automatically will work against you. You must be a realist, that is, you must base your life on facts and not on anything that seems imaginary, impractical, theoretical or utopian. The degree of complications in an individual's life corresponds to his insistence on dwelling on the way he thinks the world ought to be rather than the way it actually is."
—ROBERT RINGER (1938–), *Looking Out for #1* (Fawcett, 1978)

RELIGION

Religion addresses deep human anxieties. Dogma can answer the unanswerable, resolve the yearning for purpose and meaning, explain the existence of evil, and provide a set of moral rules. Against all these are the arguments of science that there is no tangible proof for the authorities of these religions and those of philosophy that there is no rational support for them. However, science is no substitute for religion. The unbelievers should take the believers more seriously, not because religious beliefs are true but because religious needs are real. Without worship, without some great context of meaning, our lives shrivel up and lack vitality. But one of the dangers of religion is that it encourages people to imagine that supernatural fantasies are facts. Religious people then claim to know the ultimate truth and try to impose their beliefs on the rest of humanity.

The Unanswerable Questions

There are two general views of what religion is. One, found in Western philosophy and some Asian religions, is that religion is a purely human invention, an attempt to explain and understand the unknown. The second view requires faith in the supernatural and the existence of supernatural beings who are believed to have created it, such as gods, angels, and devils.

The basic question to ask oneself is really this: Is it possible to explain everything that is happening to us and around us only with the laws of physics and chemistry? The strongest argument in favor of the existence of a deity is the fact that biological systems function more effectively than could be expected if based upon quantum mechanics or any other physical hypothesis. In fundamental matters a mystery remains. Even if we allow that not all of the natural laws (or laws of nature) have as yet been discovered, there are problems that we do not know how to tackle. What is the origin of the universe? Are we on this earth for a purpose? Why do we have to die?

On the other hand, a question for fundamentalists: There are three to five million different species in existence on earth today. Were all created in one day and all accommodated on the ark of Noah, as the Bible reports?

As I have said before, we have to learn how to live with questions to which, at least at the present time, there are no answers. Modern physics indicates that there are phenomena that we cannot comprehend. How can a thing be a piece of matter or just a wave? What is infinity? To answer these questions and to ward off the fear of the unknown, religions were invented. Pain and suffering also had to be acknowledged so they could be confronted. Many religions try to explain them as punishment for sinful behavior. This does not make sense. Why punish babies and animals who do not even know what sin is or that it exists?

One of the major problems that rationalism has not been able to deal with is, to quote Walter Burkert (1931–2015), that "People are quite inclined to accept their own guilt, a readiness which makes the course of events understandable and offers a way to handle or refashion one's own fate, in contrast to the oppressive burdens of chance and necessity." (In *Creation of the Sacred,* Harvard University Press, 1998).

If there is a God, then everything that happens to us has to be God's will and a realization of God's purpose. When we finally understand how the universe works, we will know the mind of God.

෧

"[C]ertain central aspects of the mind are deep mysteries that are unlikely ever to be resolved by human intelligence. The list of these mysteries is not short or trivial: sentience, the self, free will, meaning, knowledge, morality ... questions that fall into [Noam] Chomsky's category of mysteries—questions our minds are not constructed to answer as a matter of principle."
—COLIN MCGINN (1950–), reviewing *How the Mind Works*
by Steven Pinker, *TNR,* February 23, 1998

"'God' is not God's name. God is our name for that which is greater than all and yet present in each, that which illuminates and enlightens, comforts and saves."
—FORREST CHURCH (1948–2009)

"I accept the possibility of scientific explanations for almost every mystery of the natural world—but not for the greatest mystery of all. We still have no scientific answer, and expect there never to be one, to that challenge which Paul Tillich posed to me and my skeptical

classmates: 'Why is there something, when there could have been nothing?' Religion will thrive as long as there are human beings alive to reflect on the mystery of the First Cause."
—JARED DIAMOND (1937–) *NYR*, November 7, 2002

"Big things put little things in perspective. Religious people may think that they found answers to questions that can't be answered, but by simply asking them, the frame of their lives is changed."
—FORREST CHURCH (1948–2009), Sermon, May 25, 1993

"Religion: Not to believe is inconceivable—and to believe is impossible. People assume that God would provide for the troubled. But people should realize that they have only one another to fall back on."
—JEAN-JACQUES ROUSSEAU (1712–1778)

"I believe in Spinoza's God, who reveals himself in the orderly harmony of what exists, not in a God who concerns himself with fates and actions of human beings."
—ALBERT EINSTEIN (1879–1955)

"There are three modes of bearing the ills of life: by indifference, by philosophy and by religion." (FB: Or by complaining.)
—CHARLES CALEB COLTON (1780–1832)

"Religion is the sigh of the oppressed and an expression of indignation by the sick and poor."
—KARL MARX (1818–1883)

"The various modes of worship which prevailed in the Roman world were all considered by the people as equally true; by the philosopher as equally false; and by the magistrate as equally useful. And thus toleration produced not only mutual indulgence, but even religious concord."

—EDWARD GIBBON (1737–1794), *History of the Decline and Fall of the Roman Empire*

"Religion is our human response to the dual mystery of being alive and having to die. ... Knowing that we are going to die, we tend to ask ourselves what life means."

—FORREST CHURCH (1948–2009), Sermon, April 19, 1992

Religion v. Science

The basic antithesis between religion and science is this: religion believes that 1) the truth has been revealed; 2) instructions on how to lead the good life have been given; 3) doubting is abhorred—what we have received from our gods or teachers has to be preserved. Science 1) believes that little is known; 2) attempts through reason to find out how the universe works; 3) doubts the truth of statements that cannot be proven.

Science is essentially descriptive, describing what exists and explaining how it works. Science may define outcomes, but it cannot judge what the best outcome is. On the other hand, philosophy is essentially based on prescriptive analysis, which requires value judgments.

Physicists try to deal with situations that can be analyzed. They look for simple situations that illustrate the basic principles clearly. T. D. Rogers said that "science proceeds not by asking the big question 'What is the nature of mind?' but by asking the little question 'What happens to Joe Snooks's mind when he is hit over the head by a crowbar?'" (*The Lancet,* July 23, 1994) (FB: Philosophy asks the big questions.)

Richard Feynman (1918–1988) said that science is about not what we know but what we don't know. That is what it has in common with religion. Science appeals to the head and religion to the heart. We must make science appeal to both the head and the heart.

When thinking about religion, if we succeed in freeing ourselves temporarily of our anxieties and hopes, we will find ourselves speculating, as E. H. Jellinek noted (in *The Lancet*, December 23, 2000), whether "abiogenesis (or archebiosis)—that is, the process by which living matter had come into being independently of pre-existing living matter in the distant past—was still going on." Or was it terminated at the end of the creation? According to Maimonides (1135–1204), "The foundation of our faith is the belief that God created the Universe from nothing; that time did not exist previously but was created."

The black hole question: a black hole is an area of space so dense with matter that gravity traps even light, preventing it from escaping to any outside observer. In *A Brief History of Time* (Random House, 1988), Stephen Hawking (1942–) showed that within each black hole there must also be a singularity, a place where space, time, and matter are crushed to a single point. However, he claims it is possible that the universe did not begin with a singularity. Instead, space and time may have no boundaries at all:

"The universe would be completely self-contained and not affected by anything outside itself. It would neither be created nor destroyed. It would just BE. … [This idea] has profound implications for the role of God in the affairs of the universe. … So long as the universe had a beginning, we could suppose it had a creator. But if the universe is really completely self-contained with no boundary or edge, it would have neither beginning nor end. … What place then, for a creator? … With the success of scientific theories in describing events, most people have come to believe that God allows the universe to evolve according to a set of laws and does not intervene in the universe to break these laws."

అ

"The story that we have in the West, so far as it is based on the Bible, is based on a view of the universe that belongs to the first millennium BC. It does not accord with our concept either of the universe or of the dignity of man. It belongs entirely somewhere else."
—Joseph Campbell (1904–1987), *Myths to Live By* (Penguin, 1993)

"The history of science is the history of the battle of reason against revealed truth (in which I would include political ideologies such as Marxism).
—François Jacob (1920–2016), *Of Flies, Mice and Men*
(Harvard University Press, 1998)

"After confrontations such as that with Galileo, Christianity accepted the autonomy of reason and gave up trying to control science. Hostile to the notion of human rights after the French Revolution, Christianity now accepts and promotes them."
—Leszek Kolakowski (1927–2009), quoted by Nathan Gardels,
NPQ, Fall/Winter 2009/2010

"The primary problem is not to provide the public with the knowledge of how far it is to the nearest star and what genes are made of … the problem is to get them to reject irrational and supernatural explanations of the world, the demons that exist only in their imaginations. … The reason people do not have a correct view of nature is not that they are ignorant of this or that fact about the material world, but that they look to the wrong sources in their attempt to understand."

> — RICHARD LEWONTIN (1929–), reviewing Carl Sagan's
> *The Demon-Haunted World, NYR,* January 9, 1997
> Copyright © 1997 by Richard Lewontin

"What really interests me is whether God had any choice in the creation of the world."

> —ALBERT EINSTEIN (1879–1955)

Faith v. Reason

The conflict between reason and faith is the major issue dividing atheism from theism. George H. Smith (1949–) in *Atheism: The Case Against God* (Nash, 1974) writes that "Faith means acting without critical deliberation ... acting because it is demanded of one by an authority. ... If there is a uniform theme throughout the Bible it is that God must be obeyed. ... God is the master, man is the slave, and ... a slave is not permitted to act according to his own judgment. ... Obedience is a convenient escape from taking individual responsibility."

In *Judaism, Human Values and the Jewish State* (Harvard University Press, 1992), Yeshayahu Leibowitz (1903–1994) says faith is not a conclusion but an "evaluative decision that one makes, and like all evaluations, it does not result from any information one has acquired, but is a commitment to which one binds himself. ... Faith is the supreme, if not the only, manifestation of a man's free choice." Leibowitz denies that religion makes any truth claims whatsoever about the nature of the universe. He solves the problem of religion and science by declaring that the two operate in entirely independent spheres. "Science makes no claims about how we ought to behave, religion makes no claims about how we ought to believe and thus, therefore, cannot possibly come into conflict."

❧

"I think it is impossible to explain faith. It is like trying to explain air, which one cannot do by dividing it into its component parts and labeling them scientifically. It must be breathed to be understood."

—PATRICK WHITE (1912–1990), quoted by Andrew Sullivan from *Patrick White: A Life* by David Marr, *NYT*, March 22, 1992

"Faith is a state of mind that leads people to believe in something—it does not really matter what—without a whisper of doubt or a wisp of evidence, and believe it so strongly in some cases they are prepared to kill and die for it without the need for further justification. ... [It] is powerful enough to immunize people against all appeals to pity, to forgiveness, to decent human feeling. It can even immunize them against fear."

—RICHARD DAWKINS (1941–), *New Humanist*, May 1989

"We do not have too much intellect and too little soul, but too little intellect in matters of the soul."

—ROBERT MUSIL (1880–1942)

"The Christian religion not only was at first attended with miracles, but even at this day cannot be believed by any reasonable person without one."

—DAVID HUME (1711–1776)

Evil

The biggest problem in life is to understand and comprehend the existence of evil. Actions, events or experiences become evil when they horrify us and when we cannot make sense of them—evil challenges our hope that the world makes sense. Susan Neiman's (1955–) *Evil in Modern Thought* (Princeton University Press, 2002) raises the questions, "Can there be meaning in a world where innocents suffer? Can belief in divine power or human progress survive a cataloging of evil?"

The reality of evil is never denied in the Bible, but there is no explanation in it for the existence of evil. Evil is under the rule of God. The forces of goodness and evil, according to the Bible, are not equal. Evil comes into existence only in opposition to good; evil is derivative, not sui generis. Thus, as long as there is no explanation for the existence of evil there can be no certainty about the existence of God.

Christianity imposes the awesome responsibility of working out some sort of theodicy—the philosophical attempt "to justify the ways of God to man," as Milton (1608–1674) wrote. It attempts to vindicate the divine attributes (e.g., goodness) in the face of the existence of physical and moral evil. How could an all-loving and all-powerful God create a world in which evil exists, with the injustices, the pain, the cruelties, the humiliations? The Christian doctrine has the answers: We were conceived and born in sin, and we share in the guilt passed down from generation to generation since Adam's original sin in Eden.

The Episcopal litany asks for deliverance "from all evil and wickedness, from sin, from the crafts and assaults of the devil, from thy wrath and from everlasting damnation." The Catholic baptismal sponsor swears in the name of the child to "reject Satan, father of sin and prince of darkness." C. S. Lewis (1898–1963) said, "There is no neutral ground in the universe: every square inch, every split second, is claimed by God and counterclaimed by Satan." We must choose.

Maimonides (1135–1204) said God has not made evil. God gave us the power to manage evil.

Evil is not a satanic force coming from outside the human race; it is a misapplication of human powers, a failure of human capacities. It derives from human potential, not a supernatural force.

&

"It is the fate of those who toil at the lower employments of life, to be rather driven by the fear of evil, than attracted by the prospect of good."
—Samuel Johnson (1709–1784)

"The religious answer to the existence of evil: God sees the truth but waits."
—Dostoevsky (1821–1881)

"The point of view of the religious person is: it is not within our ability to understand or explain the tranquil well-being of the wicked or the afflictions of the righteous."
—Irving Bunim, *Ethics from Sinai*, Vol. 2 (Philipp Feldheim, 1966)

"All evil arises from man's inability to sit still."
—Blaise Pascal (1623–1662)

"When one looks around and sees all the misery and injustice and evil, one has to doubt the existence of just, good and powerful deities.

But then something happens that makes you believe in them. I just returned home from the funeral of one of my enemies."

—SENECA (4 BCE–65 CE)

Setting Moral Laws and Rules

It is a basic human need to interpret one's own life in moral terms. The question is whether this can be done in the framework of common sense and reason without the help of revelation. I do not believe that one has to invoke God to do what is morally right. We must have independent standards of goodness.

Judaism, Christianity, and Islam insist on a God-centered view of the world and impose demands for a life lived under the constraints of divine law.

Christians also believe that divine law, i.e., something proceeding from God (revealed law), is the foundation of liberty and the safeguard against tyranny. But the Western liberal tradition comes not from Judeo-Christianity but from Greece, in particular from its questioning approach to life. Above all, democracy and the open society, science and philosophy, came from Greece.

The common requirement of fundamentalist belief is that biblical statements—on creation, evolution, and punishment for sins of ancestors—be taken literally and without question.

There is a clear message about punishment. The descendants of Noah—the entirety of post-flood humanity—who were "all of one language and of one speech" (Genesis 11), decided to build a tower reaching to heaven. Their plan so offended God that he decided to "confuse their language." Unable to communicate, the builders had to halt construction.

જ

"I remain uneasy about relying on religion to justify morality; today, as in the past, it's too small a step from there to justifying the killing of adherents of other religions."

—JARED DIAMOND (1937–), *NYR*, November 7, 2002

"Religion has great significance because with it, one's entire social and private life is no longer guided by instinct but by ethical norms which become more necessary the more involved and complicated the collective condition of the civilized world becomes."

—T. G. MASARYK (1850–1937), *Suicide and the Meaning of Civilization*, published in 1879

"Let us not forget that the central Christian doctrine is that man committed the original sin and that the death of the son of God atoned for the sins of man."

—EDWARD O. WILSON (1929–), *Consilience: The Unity of Knowledge* (Knopf, 1998)

"God does not punish us; we punish ourselves. Those who are in hell are there by their own choice. They could walk right out of it if they so choose, except that their values are such as to make the path out of hell appear dangerous, painful and impossibly difficult."

—M. SCOTT PECK (1936–2005), *People of the Lie* (Simon & Schuster, 1985)

"Appreciate the ruthless consistency of primary Christian virtues—such as humility, self-sacrifice and a sense of sin—which, without exception, are geared to the destruction of man's inner sense of dignity, efficacy and personal worth. ... Christianity must destroy reason before it can introduce faith, so it must destroy happiness before it can introduce salvation."

—GEORGE H. SMITH (1949–) *Atheism: The Case Against God*
(Nash, 1974)

Aspects of Specific Religions

A. J. Carlson (1875–1956) noted in *Science,* February 27, 1931, that "Neither Jesus nor his apostles appear to have claimed any supernatural authority or absolute wisdom for their sayings or writings. The ignoble doctrine of divine revelation of absolute truth for all times appears to be a later invention. But in Mormonism and Mohammedanism it is present with the founders."

The Quakers or the Religious Society of Friends find their principles in "No Cross, No Crown," a tract by William Penn (1644–1718). Among them are the worth of all people, including the poor and powerless, the immigrants, the undocumented and the refugees, the homeless and the unemployed. All life is sacred—that of the oppressed and the oppressor. The world is one community. Work for peace, justice, and tolerance, giving silent help from the nameless to the nameless. The underlying philosophy: to help people help themselves, avoiding the quick fix and the imposition of outside ideas about what an individual or community needs.

Celibacy was not an original rule of the Catholic Church, although it had been practiced in various orders and circumstances. In the eleventh century, Pope Gregory VII, who feared that priests' progeny would inherit ecclesiastical property, launched a ruthless campaign against clerical marriage that divested priests of their wives and children.

Zen and other Eastern religions advocate self-contemplation as the key to understanding the universe. To believe in Zen, one has to see oneself emptied of the demands of meaning. In Zen, said French philosopher Roland Barthes (1915–1980), there is "an excision which removes the flourish of meaning from the object and severs from its presence, from its position in the world, any tergiversation (i.e., equivocation)."

The essence of Zen is acceptance. One is as one is. Let be what is. It is here and now. When hungry, eat. When sleepy, sleep.

The evolution of Hinduism, according to J. M. Coetzee (1940–) in his review of *Half a Life* by V. S. Naipaul (*NYR*, November 1, 1991): "Asceticism: fasting, celibacy, silence. Why do people make self-denial their central religious practice, in India in particular, and what are the human consequences? ... Hindu temples, as a result of foreign invasions, lost their revenues. ... Poverty led to loss of energy and desire, which led to passivity, which led to deeper poverty. ... Instead of quitting temple life, the caste came up with a transvaluation of values: not eating and denial of the appetites in general were propagated as admirable in themselves, worthy of veneration."

In *The Power of Myth* with Bill Moyers (1934–), Joseph Campbell (1904–1987) described nirvana as "a state of mind or consciousness, not a place ... the state you find when you are no longer driven to live by compelling desires, fears and social commitments." (Doubleday, 1988)

Many African religions draw no sharp distinction between the natural world and human beings. The creator is not separate from the created. The entire process of nature relates to God.

જ

"I teach only two things: the cause of human sorrow and the way to become free of it."

—Buddha (563–483 BCE)

"An integral part of Puritanism is its disdainful view of the behavior of others."

—Daniel E. Koshland, Jr. (1920–1987), *Science*, June 1, 1990

"Islam, like Christianity and Judaism, contains within itself the seeds of extremism and violence."

—Malise Ruthven (1942–), *A Fury for God* (Granta Books, 2002)

"There are some religions which are very malign on almost any criteria, and no society has ever found it very easy to draw a clear line between respectable religions and malign ones."

—Don Cupitt (1934–)

Humanism v. Traditional Religion

Traditional religion does not speak to the problems of our age. Revelation without substantiation is what traditional religion is all about.

Religion should not teach doctrines that lead to suffering, e.g., refusing birth control. Our ultimate commitment has to be to human beings and not to ideas or ideologies.

Humanism is a philosophy or way of life, not a religion. It is a secular force for justice and enlightenment. It does not aspire to put a man in God's place. Humanism cannot answer some of the deepest questions about the moral life, such as how to come to terms with evil, why virtue is not rewarded, and why evil is not punished.

Humanists believe that liberty and freedom from tyranny are basic human rights. Humans, although unequal in endowments and aptitudes, are all of equal value.

The essence of Humanism is not life; it lies in the understanding of what gives life value.

ॐ

"A religion [is] a set of theories about entities that are not observable by physical means ... [whereas] a philosophy such as secular humanism must be based on postulates grounded in reality."
—MILTON ROTHMAN (1919–2001), *Free Inquiry*, Winter 1992/1993

"The basis of humanism is the recognition that human beings are both the same but different: that there is not only nothing above the human but there should be no human above another human, that myself and other selves have equal value, that the differences between us are part of our common humanity, and that a good society should recognize this and be consciously pluralist."
—NICOLAS WALTER (1934–2000), *New Humanist*, March 1991

S

SCIENCE

The purpose of science is to change the world. Its essential nature is to discover the truth, formulate it, and make it a matter of public knowledge.

Philosopher Bernard Williams (1929–2003) said, "scientific realism [is] the concept that there is a world independent of our inquiry to which our inquiry has to be faithful, and that....it is the business of science to try to...arrive at a description of the world which any other competent inquirer—even from another galaxy—could, in principle, converge on." (*The Center Magazine*, November/December 1983)

Science:
- is the study of verifiable facts, not of beliefs or expectations.
- is objective—free of subjective, nonrational value judgments.
- is concerned with the great discoveries of general laws and influences not perceptible to our senses.
- has as its goal to discover how the universe works. It is not a collection of facts, just as a pile of bricks is not a house. Science tries to understand how the facts hang together. It does this by formulating hypotheses and testing their ability to predict events.
- has measurement as its method. You can measure only what has already happened or what is happening. One cannot measure future events; one can only predict them based on measurements of what has happened.

- should reduce the description of more complex phenomena to that of simpler ones. It should also reveal the mechanical laws that validate seemingly random events.
- is a process of discovery rather than invention. Literature is invention.

ൟ

"Doubt is not to be feared but welcomed. ... Science is a way to teach how something gets to be known, what is not known, to what extent things *are* known (for nothing is known absolutely), how to handle doubt and uncertainty, what the rules of evidence are, how to think about things so that judgments can be made, how to distinguish truth from fraud, and from show."
—RICHARD FEYNMAN (1918–1988), quoted by James Gleick in *Genius: The Life and Science of Richard Feynman* (Pantheon, 1992)

"The only solid piece of scientific truth about which I feel totally confident is that we are profoundly ignorant about nature. Indeed, I regard this as the major discovery of the past 100 years of biology."
—LEWIS THOMAS (1913-1993), *The Medusa and the Snail* (Viking, 1979)

Natural Laws

In *Consilience: The Unity of Knowledge* (Knopf, 1998), Edward O. Wilson (1929–) makes the assumption that "all tangible phenomena ... are based on material processes that are ultimately reducible to the laws of physics."

All objects, whether celestial or terrestrial, organic or inorganic, are uniformly governed by the same set of natural laws, including the laws of gravity, thermodynamics, and many others. The problem is that we do not know all of the natural laws. In dealing with particles and their modes of aggregation, for instance, their behavior follows certain laws, the knowledge of which permits us to make predictions.

What distinguishes living organisms from nonliving objects? Can all natural phenomena ultimately be explained in terms of physics and chemistry? Is biology reducible to chemistry?

Yes. We no longer need any new principles transcending the existing framework of physics and chemistry to explain living phenomena. DNA research has brought to an end the long history of vitalistic speculations.

Nor does asserting that the whole may be more than the sum of its parts mean the explanation of biological phenomena in terms of physics and chemistry is unsound. For instance, the ant colony as a whole does have a kind of knowledge—how to grow, how to move, how to build—that cannot be found in the individual ant. Ant colonies have been with us for 300 million years. Instead of creative intelligence, they have patterns of behavior.

ॐ

"There is a real world independent of our senses; the laws of nature were not invented by man, but forced upon him by that natural world. They are the expression of a rational world order."

—MAX PLANCK (1858–1947), *The Philosophy of Physics*
(Norton, 1936)

"One should always hold it more likely that one has been deceived than that the laws of nature should stand suspended."

—DAVID HUME (1711–1776)

Relativity, Complementarity, Uncertainty

The concept of relativity expresses the essential dependence of physical phenomena on the frame of reference used for their coordination in space and time. The notion of complementarity—the concept that the underlying properties of entities may manifest themselves in contradictory forms at different times (i.e., light sometimes exhibits properties of waves and sometimes properties of particles) serves to symbolize our ingrained idea that phenomena exist independently of the means by which they are observed.

The Heisenberg uncertainty principle, formulated by Werner Heisenberg (1901–1976), claims that it is impossible to specify precisely and simultaneously the position and velocity of particles. Yet it cannot be used to abandon the validity of the laws of physics and chemistry. Indeterminism is present only at the level of submicroscopic particles; at the macroscopic level of ordinary objects, the deterministic laws of physics still apply. Thus our knowledge of the present state of a particle does not permit us to predict with any certainty its future states. From this, Heisenberg concluded that quantum mechanics had destroyed the determinism of classical physics and established, in Heisenberg's term, "the final failure of causality." Heisenberg's principle is one of the most successful scientific theories: it predicts the behavior of atomic particles under specified conditions.

☙

"There is a quasi-religious Platonistic belief in an a priori realm of mathematical laws that is associated with the 'mind of God.' … The alternative position of positivism … holds that we cannot know the ultimate nature of reality. All we can know is what our observations and measurements show us. … [Theologian Keith Ward (1938–)] suggests that the mathematical laws physicists discover are 'more like descriptions of what actually happens' than they are 'mysteriously existing principles that make things happen.'"

—MARGARET WERTHEIM (1958–), *The Sciences*, March/April 1999

Unmeasurable Realities

Can science verify answers to transcendent questions? It depends on the questions. Mathematician-codebreaker Alan Turing (1912–1954) said a calculating machine could, with enough time and memory, calculate anything about the universe that was calculable. Many things in the universe, though, are not calculable, such as thoughts and feelings. The big, unsolved problem is how to find a rational, universally acceptable basis for ethics, because science cannot decide, for example, whether private property should be inherited or whether capital should belong to the state.

We measure what is measurable, often instead of what is important, because the important may not be measurable. As science deals with reality, so does non-science, which includes areas that cannot be subjected to tests of validation or refutation. Questions such as what is the purpose of life or the point of living involve individual tastes and values. Like poetry, art, and human interactions, which are not science and cannot be objectively measured, they are equally valid.

❧

"There are classes of problems to which the scientific method is inherently inapplicable. The scientific method is inapplicable to the story of history and many social sciences."
—Karl Popper (1902–1994), *The Poverty of Historicism*
(Routledge, 1960)

"Science (unlike the arts) can be detached from those who do it."
—Steve Jones (1944–), *Almost Like a Whale* (Doubleday, 2000)

"A novelist is the opposite of a mathematician. The novelist accumulates detail, he produces rich and voluptuous descriptions of reality. The mathematician does not accumulate facts but distills them. He dismisses the particular happening he is observing in favor of the abstract, the general. The calculus is an attempt to comprehend things that we take for granted. Zeno's paradox: Proving that an arrow is at rest throughout its flight because at each individual moment we can specify its location."
—David Berlinski (1942–), *A Tour of the Calculus* (Pantheon, 1995)

"I recently read a piece that said myth and fiction are as valuable as science. But a statement like that is meaningless unless you ask: Valuable for what?"
—Dudley R. Herschbach (1932–), Nobelist in chemistry

Science and Society

Man is the ultimate point of reference. Science can help us build many different kinds of structures to support life, but man must determine what kinds of structures he wants and then create them. Machines also have to be put into a civilizing context, as determined by man. Our aim is to build a world in which technological progress and efficiency will not be ends in themselves but will serve the causes of human freedom, dignity, and happiness through democratic processes.

Recent scientific and technological advances do not make previously accumulated understanding and insights unnecessary or superfluous. People and their problems will not change merely because science advances.

In the past the authorities in power tried to control through religion. Now they are trying to do it through science. According to the scientific perspective, man is viewed as a nonresponsible organism that has no powers of decision, an organism that does not act but merely displays the consequences of his impulses, drives, instincts, etc.

Scientists are accelerating the process of pumping power into a social structure which is hardly competent to contain it, and forcing the possibilities of choice upon our fellows to whom this enlarged freedom is an embarrassment. Science generates power: the megaton explosion and the ability to cure cancer are powers of exactly the same kind.

It is important that our society should not be ruled by scientists. Scientists know nothing about values. Their ability to attain recognition has no relation to their ability to formulate normative, ethical constructs or to affect public policy. This task should fall to humanists instead, because most scientists, although they may be experts in their field of knowledge, are not cultured, i.e., neither aware of nor interested in the humanities.

We cannot continue to hope that advances in science and technology will solve moral problems by themselves. Scientific findings are not value-laden; there are no moral values in Newton's laws of motion, Avogadro's number, or quantum mechanics.

᷄

"Expertise in a field of science or learning or attainment in one field does not imply wisdom, balanced judgment, or the ability to enjoy life. People matter more than concepts and must come first. The worst of all despotisms is the heartless tyranny of ideas."
—PAUL JOHNSON (1928–), *Intellectuals*
(HarperCollins, 1989)

"Concern for man himself and his fate must always form the chief interest of all technical endeavors."
—ALBERT EINSTEIN (1879–1955)

"Scientific knowledge should be pursued in the context of social relevance. Science should serve mankind. Scientific education should be improved to allow this to happen."
— LANCELOT HOGBEN (1895–1975), quoted by Sarah Bundery,
The Lancet, February 14, 1998

"The scientific advances of the nineteenth century and the first half of the twentieth were generally beneficial to society as a whole, spreading wealth to rich and poor alike ... The electric light, the telephone, the refrigerator, radio, television, synthetic fabrics, antibiotics, vitamins and vaccines were social equalizers. ... During the last forty years ... the strongest efforts in applied science have been concentrated upon products that can be profitably sold."
—FREEMAN DYSON (1923–), *Imagined Worlds*
(Harvard University Press, 1998)

"No one can predict the use of scientific knowledge. ... Scientists have one main obligation: to make public the implications, wherever possible, of their work. ... They cannot take responsibility for the way their discoveries are used." (FB: That is the responsibility of the government or society. Restrictions may be necessary.)
—LEWIS WOLPERT (1929–), *The Lancet,* January 30, 1993

"Biology has a dismal history of being used to absolve murderers, rapists, thieves, martyrs, saints, capitalists, communists and social democrats from blame for their actions."
—STEVE JONES (1944–), reviewing *Why Is Sex Fun?* by Jared Diamond, *NYR,* July 17, 1997

Research

The basic nature of the scientist, as opposed to the technologist, is the fascination of finding out how nature, and the rest of the universe, actually works; disinterested curiosity, in fact. Derek de Solla Price (1922–1983) said in 1980: "The product of a scientist is a paper; the product of a technologist is a process."

Although the research attitude classically defies orthodoxy, wrestles with status quo, and shuns appeals to authority, many discoveries brought about by the application of the scientific method were not the object of scientific research but side benefits.

We need basic research to understand the world around and inside us. It is of the utmost importance not to focus all our energies on solving specific problems. For example, the new cancer remedies do not come to us as a result of cancer research, but from investigations of what governs the normal procession of cell growth and division of simple organisms, such as baker's yeast, fruit flies, and earthworms.

In *Behavioral Science* (January 1990), J. V. Brady (1922–2011) described using a research approach "with its roots in environmentalism which has two main features: 1) knowledge comes from experience rather than innate ideas, divine revelations or other obscure sources; and 2) action is governed by consequences rather than instinct, reason, will, belief, attitudes, or even the currently fashionable cognitions." Psychology and the social sciences should be based on the same principles.

Politics and public policy must reflect both the best that science has to offer and the broader socioeconomic values society sets as its priorities. Knowledge, although important, may be less important to a decent society than the way it is obtained. Thus the paramount rights of subjects in clinical research are 1) their welfare and 2) the right to refuse to participate. When doing medical research abroad, the same ethical standards enforced in the United States have to apply. According to the World Medical Association Declaration of Helsinki, 1964: "Concern for the interests of the subject must always prevail over the interests of science and society."

಄

"The development of Western science has been based on two great achievements, the invention of the formal, logical system (in Euclidean geometry) … and the discovery of the possibility of finding out causal relationships by systematic experiment."

—ALBERT EINSTEIN (1879–1955)

"The difficult trick in the art and craft of science is to exercise discipline while still obeying one's daimon."

—ROBERT K. MERTON (1910–2003)

"The motto of England's Royal Society is *Nullius in verba*: Trust not in words. Observation and experiment are what count, not opinion and introspection."
—STEVE JONES (1944 –), *NYR*, November 6, 1997

"How odd it is that anyone should not see that all observation must be for or against some view if it is to be of any service."
—CHARLES DARWIN (1809–1882)

"Identify a valid scientific proposition by whether it is stated in a form in which it could possibly be disproved or rejected. If a theory is too general or flexible—such as that people born under the sign of Leo tend to be temperamental—to be proven wrong, it is incapable of generating new knowledge."
—KARL POPPER (1902–1994)

"Anything requiring a calculation to determine its statistical significance isn't obvious enough."
—THOMAS HUNT MORGAN (1866–1945), who worked out the universal genetic mechanisms using fruit flies

"By the misuse of language and logic, observed associations are presented as causal links."
—J. S. MCCORMICK, *PBM* 35, 1992

"A study is ethical or not at its inception; it does not become ethical because it succeeds in producing valuable data."
—HENRY K. BEECHER, MD (1904–1976), *JAMA*, January 3, 1966

"Virtually any type of data is amenable to … interpretation. For example, interview observations can be coded quantitatively (patient appears withdrawn (1) yes, (2) no). It is thereby possible to incorporate qualitative observations and quantitative data into the predictive mix."

—Robyn M. Dawes, David Faust, Paul E. Meehl,
Science, March 31, 1989

"There is no room for 'consequentialism,' the idea that all that counts morally are the consequences of one's actions. Data must not be omitted because they do not support a theory."

—Ruth Millikan, PhD (1933–), *American Scholar*, 60:505, 1991

"Every attempt an individual makes to solve problems that affect all of us is bound to fail. ... The content of biology is the concern of biologists, its effects the concern of all men. What concerns all can only be worked out by all. ... Knowledge cannot be kept secret."

—Friedrich Duerrenmatt (1921–1990), *The Physicists* (play)
(Grove Press, 1964)

"If there is any single influence that will take the life of scientific research, it will be secrecy and enforced confidentiality. ... A good deal of scientists ... have never learned how to avoid waffling when yes or no are not available and the only correct answer is, 'I don't know.'"

—Lewis Thomas (1913–1993), *Discover*, November 1983

SUCCESS

- The secret of success is to get up when you fall down.
- Winning without waging a battle is the key to success.
- We cannot achieve what we cannot imagine.

There is no set of facts that will induce success. To succeed, we have to be able to choose the relevant facts. But we need guidelines and ground rules. We have to set goals and define ways to attain them.

❧

"It is not enough to aim, you must hit."

—ITALIAN PROVERB

"The two things that make for success in life are: 1) bridging the gap between intention and achievement and 2) distinguishing between information which empowers and information which merely informs. … We have to come from what we really want rather than come from merely what seems possible. … Mastery is the capacity to operate successfully beyond a particular paradigm, process or point of view."

—WERNER ERHARD (1935–)

"Don't ever get efforts confused with results. The world operates on results."

—JEAN-BAPTISTE COLBERT (1619–1683)

"Success in life depends rather upon habits of industry and attention to business details than upon knowledge."

—SAMUEL SMILES (1812–1904)

"Success breeds success. Being part of a successful team is what it is all about."

—SIR HUGH STEVENSON (1942 –)

"I think that success is often a function of figuring out what you are good at and building your life around it."

—ALAN DERSHOWITZ (1938–)

"Feynman kept emphasizing that the key to his achievements was not anything 'magical' but the right attitude, the focus on nature's reality, the focus on asking the right questions, the willingness to try (and to discard) unconventional answers, the sensitive ear for phoniness, self-deception, bombast, and conventional but unproven assumptions."
—JAMES GLEICK (1954–), *Genius: The Life and Science of Richard Feynman* (Pantheon, 1992)

"Every man has the right to be conceited, until he is successful."
—BENJAMIN DISRAELI (1804–1881)

"Nothing recedes like success."
—WALTER WINCHELL (1897–1972)

"There is only one success—to be able to spend your own life in your own way."
—CHRISTOPHER MORLEY (1890–1957)

T

TRUTH

People tell the truth at their own pace. Truth can best be discovered with the help of reason.

The postmodernist notions that historical data are relative, all truth is subjective, and one man's narrative is as good as another's are just not so. Postmodern relativists believe not in truth but in many truths, exemplifying the gap, even crisis, between two different generations, perspectives, and sets of values. On the other hand, attacks are directed at civil libertarians, feminists, and anyone else on the wrong side of the right-wing culture war. These morality contests are really about confrontations between cultures that have different ways of interpreting virtue and villainy.

Often there is no single truth, because perceptions depend so heavily on subjective definitions and because attitudes may be deeply ambivalent.

There are eternal truths and truths of the moment.

❧

"Truth comes out of error more readily than out of confusion."
—Francis Bacon (1561–1626)

"Detecting error is the primary virtue, not proving truth."
—Karl Popper (1902–1994)

"Skepticism is the most efficacious stance that human beings can adopt with regard to any kind of knowledge."
—Bertrand Russell (1872–1970)

"What has not been examined impartially has not been well-examined. Skepticism is therefore the first step toward truth."
—Denis Diderot (1713–1784)

"A fact never went into partnership with a miracle. Truth scorns the assistance of wonders. A fact will fit every other fact in the universe, and that is how you can tell whether it is or is not a fact. A lie will not fit anything except another lie."
—Robert G. Ingersoll (1833–1899)

"One should be permitted to identify error without being required to correct it. If a man is drowning in his own nonsense, you should pull him out first, before you start teaching him how to swim. Even if you do not know how to swim, or how to teach swimming, you still have to pull him out. Ignorance is preferable to dogma. Truth is not decided by a majority vote."
—Petr Skrabanek (1940–1994), *PBM*, Autumn 1986

"We humans can only take so much myth-shattering at one time, so I won't press the point."
—William F. Schulz (1949–), *The World: Journal of the Unitarian Universalist Association*, May-June 1988

W

WINE, IMBIBING, TOASTS

Dr. Berger did not give his own views on wines or spirits in the notebooks, but did include these selections from others.

❧

Set down the wine and the dice and perish the thought of tomorrow.

—VIRGIL (70–19 BCE)

"We have to exaggerate to focus attention on essentials. Yet, as with all fine things and wines, one comes to appreciate their rarity only by tasting the many others."

—M. THERESE SOUTHGATE, MD (1928–2013), *JAMA*, May 22, 1996

"Where there is no wine, drugs are useful."

—THE TALMUD

"I often wonder what the vintners buy one half so precious as the goods they sell."

— EDWARD FITZGERALD (1809–1883), tr., *Rubáiyát of Omar Khayyám*

"I cannot live without champagne. In victory we deserve it, in defeat we need it."

—WINSTON CHURCHILL (1874–1965)

"What is man, when you come to think upon him, but a minutely set, ingenious machine for turning, with infinite artfulness, the red wine of Shiraz into urine?"

—Isak Dinesen (1885–1962), *Seven Gothic Tales* (Vintage, 1972)

"The harm arises not from the use of a bad thing, but from the abuse of a very good thing."

—Abraham Lincoln (1809–1865) on whisky

"They accuse me of being a drunkard. It's a lie, for whisky can't make me drunk."

—Davy Crockett (1786–1836)

"Gay god Bacchus
To thee I pray
Grant me this
For a perfect day
A genial thirst
My liquor neat
The head always
To keep my feet.
And when all's said
And drunk and done
Ability to hold my tongue."

—Julie Redmond, *Gay, Grave and Otherwise: Poems*
(Brentano's, 1949)

"Here is to our coffins. May they be made from oaks 100 years old whose acorns are planted tonight."

—Jim Miller's Toast

"Salut, amore, pesetas:
Health, love and money
And time to enjoy them."

—Walter Alvarez's Toast

"The horse and mule live thirty years, and nothing know of wine or beers.
The goat and sheep at twenty die and never taste of scotch or rye.
The cow drinks water by the ton, and at eighteen is mostly done.
The dog at fifteen cashes in, without the aid of rum or gin.
The cat in milk and water soaks, and then in twelve short years it croaks.
The modest, sober, bone-dry hen lays eggs for nogs, then dies at ten.
All animals are strictly dry; they sinless live and swiftly die.
But sinful, ginfull, rum-soaked men, survive for three score years and ten.
And some of us, though mighty few, stay pickled 'til we're 92!"

—Traditional Toast

WORK

Work has to be meaningful to make you happy.

High pay and long vacations are not satisfactory substitutes for satisfaction on the job.

The intensity of involvement in one's work makes for success and satisfaction. But it is a rare gift, a frame of mind and not simply the result of training.

If you are not enthusiastic about what you are doing, you are probably doing the wrong thing.

The old Protestant work ethic has to be replaced, where the goal of life is salvation in the afterlife and the aim of work is to contribute to God's glory. This translates as two virtues: the virtue of accumulating rather than spending and that of work as a means of purifying the self against the sinful pleasures of the body.

The secret of many successful people is that they can learn on the job. Some of the greatest contributions in science, education, business, and industry have been made by the dilettantes, people who lacked formal education in the field and had no significant prior experience but were able to identify what was missing and find a solution.

Work creates talent, concluded Nobelist Santiago Ramón y Cajal (1852–1934), often considered the father of modern neuroscience. He observed that "the plasticity of the brain allowed for improving and refining its machinery so that with experience one would become better and better at scientific thinking. ... Discoveries are made by people and not by scientific instruments or overflowing libraries." (Quoted by Jon Kaas in *Science*, June 25, 1999)

❧

"One can live magnificently in this world, if one knows how to work and how to love, to work for the person one loves, and to love one's work."

—Tolstoy (1828–1910)

"Get completely absorbed in your task, working as if obsessed. This will lift you from a horrible and objectively hopeless existence so that subjectivity will be completely lost in the object. For Schopenhauer this is the ultimate state that a human can achieve. This works only if the task and the ability are completely balanced. An overwhelming task creates anxiety. An ability that outweighs the task leads to boredom."

—George Klein (1925–2016), *The Atheist and the Holy City*
(MIT Press, 1990)

"Work gives them the comfortable illusion of existing, even of being important. If they stopped working, they'd realize they simply were not there at all, most of them. Just holes in the air, that's all."

—ALDOUS HUXLEY (1894–1963), *Point Counter Point,* 1928

"Work is more fun than about anything else."

—WARREN BUFFETT (1930–), Berkshire Hathaway Annual Meeting, 1994

Index of Sources

www.ingramcontent.com/pod-product-compliance
Lightning Source LLC
LaVergne TN
LVHW091214080426
835509LV00009B/986